D1582732

THE WOODPECKER'S HOME
CULVERLEA

THE OPEN-AIR BOY

BY

THE REV. G. M. A. HEWETT, M.A.
OF WINCHESTER COLLEGE

WINCHESTER :
WARREN AND SON LTD., 85 HIGH STREET

P. AND G. WELLS, COLLEGE STREET

All rights reserved

MADE AND PRINTED
IN GREAT BRITAIN
BY
WARREN AND SON LIMITED
THE WYKEHAM PRESS
WINCHESTER

1928

CONTENTS

LIST OF ILLUSTRATIONS

———

PREFACE

THIS book, originally published by Messrs. George Allen in 1901 and too long out of print, is now re-published, as an affectionate tribute to his memory, by the wish, and with the help, of some old friends of the author. The following obituary notice was written by one of them, A. G. Bather, only a few weeks before his own last illness began, for the *Wykehamist* of December 20th, 1927. It would be hard to find a more fitting Introduction.

GEORGE MOTTRAM A. HEWETT.

On Saturday, November 26th, there passed away, after a long and painful illness, one whom many generations of Wykehamists will remember with more than ordinary gratitude and affection. For thirty-four years Mottram Hewett was a master at Winchester, for twenty housemaster of Culverlea.

Educated at Bromsgrove School and Pembroke College, Cambridge, he came here in 1882 : he was ordained in 1884, and in 1895 he married. At the end of the same year he took over from Mr. Phillips the House Mastership of Culverlea, which he held till his retirement in 1916.

From his first years here he won for himself, both among the staff and in the School, a position peculiarly his own. Not only was he a most successful teacher with a rare understanding of the mentality of the average boy ; but out of School his life was one of many infectious activities. Chief among these was, perhaps, his devotion to Natural History in various fields : called upon to form and to take charge of that section in Museum (which was as yet unbuilt) he made himself a real authority on the birds, the butterflies and the botany of Hampshire. From boyhood he had been the keenest of observers and lovers of open-air nature ; but it was only now that he set himself to acquire that knowledge, which was later so great a help to others. By means of expeditions by night and day, in an incredibly short time he formed those collections which are now some of the treasures of our Museum. And there were other interests besides : cricket, in which on more than one occasion his bowling helped the City Club to win the Hampshire Cup ; singing in choir and Glee Club and in the Test Valley concerts ; a first-rate skater, he was one of the pioneers of Winter Sports in Switzerland ; as a fisherman he had few equals ; shooting, and every form of open-air sport was the breath of life to him. Of his work as housemaster there is no need to speak here : at the time of his retirement in 1916 the columns of the *Wykehamist* contained a very true and sympathetic account of it. Enough to say that there were few members of his House who did not form for him a lifelong friendship and affection. Since his retirement he has lived at Harestock, happy, as long as his health allowed it, in his garden, his work for the Hospital and other local institutions, and in the very varied pursuits, social, sporting and literary, which interested him.

Such a bare record of Mr. Hewett's activities, long though it be, can give no adequate picture of the man. If we read his books, *The Open-Air Boy*, *The Pedagogue at Play*, and *The Autobiography of a Rat*, we can come nearer to understanding him. But to know him one must have walked and talked with him. A giant in frame, he had a heart as big. He loved the world of Nature :

to walk with him was to realise one's own blindness, as time after time he would stop to discover and to love some tiny plant or bird or butterfly, which we should never otherwise have seen. To watch him fishing on some Scotch or Devon stream was a lesson in the almost uncanny instinct and skill of the true fisherman. Shooting, whether in covert or striding over a Scotch moor, skating at Grindelwald or Winnall, one saw him a born leader by divine right of skill as well as stature. But he was happiest when inspiring others with his own enjoyments or enthusiasms : he wanted others to share his clean enjoyment of God's world. He loved children and was loved by them. To teach a child to make a whistle out of a willow twig, to classify and name a boy's first collection of wayside flowers, meant real joy to him ; but he was no less patient and encouraging in giving the clumsiest of his middle-aged colleagues first lessons in casting a fly or figure-skating. There are many men to-day who owe some of their happiest hours and most valued interests to his teaching.

But there were other and bigger sides to his character than even these. Generous to an exceptional degree, he was careful that none but the recipients knew of his kindnesses. A scholar of rare taste, only a few of the verses he wrote are published in his books ; but many of us can remember other gems in Latin and in English. Cruelty and cant were the two things most repugnant to him. Intolerant of ceremonies, he was often outspoken to a degree which shocked the hyper-sensitive : but behind the apparent carelessness there lay a strong love and a deep reverence for the things that really mattered. His short, open advice to boys or colleagues, never given unless asked or needed, carried more weight and wisdom than many a more empassioned harangue. To the last he maintained a close interest in, and intimate knowledge of, the life of the School : and in spite of failing health and advancing years his heart was still the heart of a boy.

Was he one of those of whom he sings in the *Open-Air Boy* ?

> " Born in a mist of gold, a mist of grey
>   Enfolds our footsteps, as we creep to rest :
> And well for all who at the close of day
>   Can wonder whether gold or grey were best."

Or rather was he one who kept the boyhood and the golden glamour to the end ?

For more than thirty years Mrs. Hewett has been the most devoted partner and companion in all his work and interests. We cannot close without expressing to her the deep sympathy of all Wykehamists past and present, and their sense of a real share in her loss.

A FOREWORD

I was once a boy, and I often think how much better in every way it would be if we began at the other end. For then we should know just how long we had to live : if we were eighty to begin with, or sixty, or forty-one, we could subtract from nought, and calculate everything out nicely, and how much time to allow for it ; and we should make money first, while there was nothing better to do, and then we should spend it, when we could enjoy the spending. This would simplify the question of pocket-money at school, which is always so difficult. And so at last we should get into our cradle, and one fine day—they nearly always come when we are busy and can't enjoy them—we shouldn't be there, and there would be no bother about a funeral, nor a will either, because we should have spent all that was left while we were at school. It would be just like eating the pastry first and the mincemeat last, which I always do still when nobody is looking. But, as I say, I was once a boy, and so I know that there are three kinds of boys. The boy with a gaping mouth, with ears sticking out on each side, like a mouse-trap open. He never knows what to do, and I don't like him. Next to him I don't like the other sort, like a mouse-trap shut, and with his ears close to his head, who can learn almost anything out of a book without any bother, but is no good out of doors. But these are better, because they are only one sort of stupid. And then there is the real sort of boy, and he's the boy for whom I am writing this, so you'll find out what he's like, if you read what's coming. And I want you to read it, because I think that a lot of boys now are only men in disguise, who aren't happy unless they have a gun and a pony, and I want to show you that there are lots of things to do without having guns and ponies. In fact, the less you have guns and ponies, the longer you'll be boys, I think, and the longer you're boys the better, I think too.   And that's why I want you to read all this.   And if* anyone wants to know what I think about anything else, this will find me for a long time, I hope—

G. M. A. HEWETT,
CULVERLEA,
WINCHESTER.

---

* This invitation brought many letters, all of which he answered.   He lived 15 more years at Culverlea.

THE OPEN-AIR BOY

CHAPTER I

ANGLING MADE EASY

MY father was a wise man, and he told me two things,
and when he told you things you had to remember.
He said, " You are never to kill anything without doing
something with it, when you have killed it " ; and " You
are never to give a lot of trouble to anyone but yourself,
while you are doing something with it." He did say too,
" If you do, I'll whack you," which might count as a
third thing, for it was very important. So, because he
told me these things, I think I learnt two of the most
important lessons of my life—how to cook, and how
to keep cooks in a good temper. You can see easily, if
you try, how important these things are. For if you are
going to be out all day, half the fun is to make a fire and

cook some of the things you have killed; but in case
any accident happens, like someone coming and saying,
" You have no business to make a fire there," as they
often do, it is a very good thing to have got the cook
to give you some cold jam tart to put in your breeches
pocket. And even if nothing happens, there is always
room for both kinds of food inside you. But I shall
have to talk of these things in another chapter, and so
I only just mention them now, to show how very important I think them. First of all, then, remember two
things, one what my father said, " Don't kill things
unless you are going to do something with them," except
of course rats and mice and snails and other things that
ought to be killed, because they do mischief : and the
other is, " When you kill a thing, do it quick ; and when
you catch a thing that you are going to kill, don't wait
even a minute," because the thing may know it is going
to be killed, and then waiting is horrid. This is particularly
true when you are fishing, because you are in such a
hurry to catch another that you forget the first, which
stays flopping about and dies slow. Though if it is an
eel, as it often is, killing is very difficult and not a good
thing to talk about. But perhaps eels don't mind so
much, because they often take a walk out of the water
by themselves. At any rate the way to skin them, which
you have to do before you cook them, is to cut the head
nearly half off and then catch hold of it and pull the skin
right off down to the tail, so that it all comes off inside
out, like pulling off a stocking, and then at last you can
touch the beast without getting all over slime. Most
other fish are best killed by tapping their head against
the toe of your boot.

Now to talk about money; which always sounds
difficult, but isn't so very bad, I think, unless you are the
wrong sort of boy, who isn't happy because he hasn't

got a gun.   I'm not counting what one has at school,
because that is for the other sort of games, which I'm
not writing about.   Anyway there isn't any of it left by
the time the holidays have come.   I don't think you want
more than two shillings for each holidays, and before
you go to school five shillings for a year is enough.   I don't
think I spent quite so much as that, and I am pretty sure
that I was happier than a lot of fellows I see now, who
always seem to be growling because they have no money,
instead of setting to work and doing something.   What
one _must_ buy is a knife, which costs sixpence, with one
good blade.   This is the most expensive thing, because
one wants three a year, as they get lost rather easily.
But if you know how to be civil, as every boy ought,
you can go to the blacksmith and ask him to bore a hole
in the end, to put a string through, and when you ask
him how much it costs, he will say, " Nothing."   If he
doesn't, you will know that you haven't learnt properly
how to be civil, and you must go home and practise on
the cook or the gardener.   The latter is the best, because
he is often more like the blacksmith in temper, and can
make things nice for you in the strawberry time.   The
other end of the string goes round the nearest button
of your breeches that doesn't happen to be off.   And
this saves a knife from being lost, if you have a hole in
your pocket.   When your knife gets blunt, you rub it
on the side of a stone trough, not on one of the front-
window ledges, because it makes a great mark.   Besides
a knife, you must buy a line for fishing, which sounds
expensive, but isn't very, not more than eighteen-pence
and this will last more than a year, if you always remember
to dry it, and rub it well with dripping or fat sometimes.
This will always make a good excuse, if you get a piece
of fat at dinner which you don't like, for putting it into
your pocket, instead of being made to eat it because it

is good for you.   There is rather a lot to remember all
through this book, I know, but one soon learns to remember, and it is the next most useful thing to knowing how
to cook.   So remember also to take your line off your
rod when you've done, or else it will get into tangles,
which wears it out, especially as you want to break it
then.   When you do happen to break your line—the
easy way is to tie a knot, but it is much better, when you
get a wet day and want something to do, to ask for a
yard of silk from somebody, and to splice the line as
neatly and smartly as you can.   This sounds a bother,
but it is good for three things : because most bothers
are really good, because you may *have* to do it some day

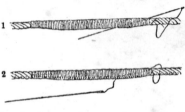

when you have a rod
with rings that a knot
sticks in, and lastly,
because, if your uncle
sees your line neatly
spliced, he may give
you a new one.   To
make a splice you lay
the broken ends together opposite ways on, a bit more
than half an inch, and then wrap the silk tightly round and
round them, not all in a lump, but beginning at the top
and finishing at the bottom.   The difficulty is with the ends.
You begin by doubling the end down about an inch,
and then wrapping over the end you have turned down
for about six rounds or more, then pull it tight and cut
it off : and you finish by threading the silk on a needle,
and wrapping about six rounds round the needle laid
alongside the line, point towards the middle of the splice,
and then pulling the needle with the loose end back under
the last six rounds and cutting the end off.

The only other thing that you *must* spend money on
is fish-hooks.   I know that the boy in most books fishes

with a bent pin ; but I tried this, when I had run out of
hooks and had no more money at present till my aunt
came, and I never could get any fish to stay on, except
one little eel who had swallowed it so far that he couldn't
get it out in time. Of course if anyone wants you to have
some more money, I should say yes, in case you might
want it, but I really don't think that you need spend it,
and it is always rather a worry for fear you lose it.

Now about the things that you want, but have to
make for yourself : at least I had to make them and they
did very well : I thought them just as good as any you
could buy. We'll begin with a rod, as we are talking
about fishing. Of course I began with a long ash-pole
that I cut in a wood, and I really don't think I ever had
anything that did better. Only the fish hadn't much
chance : I was always bigger than he was, and so he had
to be pulled out, as he couldn't pull me in. But one day
a gentleman told me that it was more like real sport for
the fish to have a chance, and showed me about umbrella
tops. So I made a real fine rod in three pieces, with pieces
of old umbrella to fit into. It was splendid fun making
it, and it certainly gave the fish a chance, as it often came
to pieces at the wrong time until I found out dodges for
making it stick, which I shan't tell you because you won't
have any fun if you don't invent some things for yourself.
So now you've got a rod and a line and a hook ; and the
next article, as they say in shops when you *do* have to
go into them, is a float. Of course anything will do as
long as it does float, such as half a cork tied on to the
line, or even a bit of stick with the line tied at each end
of it. But here's just a chance to show that you are
something better than a butcher boy, who thinks of
nothing but killing things—that if you are going to kill
things, you are going to kill them as smartly and surely
as you can, and that you can invent nice things as well as

anyone else. Besides, think what a long time you have
to watch a float, nearly an hour sometimes before anything happens, and if there is any wind to bob it about,
how difficult it is to distinguish between the wind bobbing
the float and a fish doing the same thing, only in rather

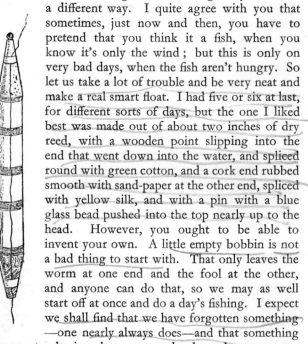

a different way. I quite agree with you that
sometimes, just now and then, you have to
pretend that you think it a fish, when you
know it's only the wind ; but this is only on
very bad days, when the fish aren't hungry. So
let us take a lot of trouble and be very neat and
make a real smart float. I had five or six at last,
for different sorts of days, but the one I liked
best was made out of about two inches of dry
reed, with a wooden point slipping into the
end that went down into the water, and spliced
round with green cotton, and a cork end rubbed
smooth with sand-paper at the other end, spliced
with yellow silk, and with a pin with a blue
glass bead pushed into the top nearly up to the
head. However, you ought to be able to
invent your own. A little empty bobbin is not
a bad thing to start with. That only leaves the
worm at one end and the fool at the other,
and anyone can do that, so we may as well
start off at once and do a day's fishing. I expect
we shall find that we have forgotten something
—one nearly always does—and that something
else wants altering, but we can do that when we come
home.

We've been writing such a long time, that it must
be too late to start to-day, and besides it is so nice to
think it all over beforehand ; one catches so many more
fish in one's mind the evening before in a cosy chair by
the fire, and so much bigger than the real ones, bigger

even than those which one nearly catches and which get
off. Well! What do you think? Ten eels of course,
two bream, four or five perch, a roach or two, and one
tench. I like tench ; they fight really well and look smart
and tidy : perch are smarter of course, but they are rather
flashy and look a bit like sham diamonds, but the nice
gentlemanly old tench looks like a well-to-do country
squire. Looking into the fire like this, I can't help thinking that we shall get one real whacker of some sort, a
bream very likely, like that five-pounder that I so nearly
got one day, when Billy (my brother) jumped in after it
and nearly got it too, it was so exhausted with pulling
against me and my ash-plant. I'm sure it was five pounds,
because I could feel it pulling and pulling for days afterwards when I shut my eyes. What time ought we to
start ? I fancy about seven o'clock myself : it's rather
fun getting up early when you aren't obliged to. So we'll
get that good cook to put us out some provisions, and
she'll give us some hot milk before we start.

Now it's all very well talking like this, but you see
I haven't the least idea what sort of country you live in,
so perhaps I'd better tell you the sort of places I went to,
and then you can choose your own according to what
you've got. You are sure to be able to find some place
to catch fish ; I never knew anyone who couldn't yet.
And even if you haven't a place, I am inclined to think
that you ought either to make one or to tell your father
that he really must go and live somewhere else.

Well, the place I liked best was what one would call
a large pond—not the sort of dirty thing with ducks on
it by a farmyard—but a clean, lonely place, where one
could see no one all day and eat one's lunch in peace.
There was a funny sort of brick tunnel at one end about
a yard above the water, where a little stream ran in, making
a sort of small waterfall. And on the left of this was a

big ash-tree hanging over the water.   Then there were
grass banks on each side with deep water below them,
and at the other end the water got gradually shallower,
till it ran away in another biggish stream.   It was very
deep under the ash-tree—so deep that I used to think
a kelpie lived there, and I daren't go near it in the evening.
There was a beautiful clump of daffodils at first under
the tree.   I was told that it was wrong to dig up wild
flowers, if there weren't many of them, though I wanted
them for my garden.   But I did dig them up at last, and
learned to swim at the same time, which is a very sad
story ; for another little boy was gathering them once
and tumbled in and was drowned.   I saw him afterwards,
and he looked so happy that I did not think it could have
hurt him.   But after that, I had to learn to swim, as it
might just as well have been me, and I was allowed to
dig up the flowers for fear anyone else, who couldn't
swim, should try to get them.   I learnt to swim rather
easily, for my father dangled me on a rope in that same
pond and almost let me go pretty often, so that I could
get used to the feel of deep water and not kick and struggle
and get excited.   I'm sure it's a better way than trying in
shallow water, where one keeps a foot on the bottom and
pretends to swim.   Anyway I advise you to learn as soon
as possible, if you can't do it already.   The great thing,
as in everything else, is to keep calm and not get flustered,
though it is not always easy.

Now let's get off—you've had your sleep, and splashed
in a bath I hope, and enjoyed your early breakfast, and
the dew is on the grass and the sun is through the haze
and everything is ripping.   But let's first think what
we've forgotten.   I know.   A bit of lead to chip a scrap
off, so that the float will stand on end.   Well do I remember
the looks of an old spout which I used for my lead quarry
or mine or wherever lead grows.   Mind you pick one

where it does not matter much. And there's one more thing—some string to make night-lines of. I'll tell you about them when we've done fishing. We've got nearly two miles to walk, so step out : don't you love being out about seven on a summer morning ? I don't mean "love getting up" ; no one does, I believe, any more in summer than in winter, but I do love being out, even in winter, when I am out for anything special, like going after wild-duck. The worst of it is I always want to go and pull everyone else out, and I did sometimes when I thought I had a reasonable chance of getting off safe. You just put a fairly wet sponge well on their face, and take a big pull at the bedclothes, and then run for all you're worth. I suppose it is the same sort of feeling which makes real good people want to make everyone else good, so it's all right to do it, only the people you do it to don't always think so. I got the wrong sort of man once, who did get up and dressed awfully quickly and came after me and spanked me and hauled me home, so I wasted a lot of time that day.

Now there's the pond, and just remember that fish are shy beasts and easily frightened. I don't think they can hear, but they feel things very quickly. So that if you stamp about on the banks, you make ripples under water, just like the rings that come when you throw a stone in, and the fish feel these and won't bite. We'll try first close under the bank, in that sort of little corner, where the water runs in from the waterfall and then runs out again. Sit down here right away from the water and get ready. I know some fellows who would walk straight up to the pond and then sit down with a bump with their legs dangling over the water, just to let the fish know they were there. Put a bit of lead, about as heavy as half a bullet, as we have a pretty heavy float, on the line about two feet above the hook. You cut a pretty deep nick in it with your knife, lay the line in the nick, and then bite it tight. Now put the float two feet above the lead, as the water is about five feet deep in that corner, and then a nice little worm. You ought to keep the worms in a cocoa-tin, with plenty of damp moss, for quite a week before you use them, and then they get pink and clean. I always dug up a few more after every day's fishing, and put them in, so that I was always sure of having a supply of good ones ready. You'll **catch** far more fish with worms like this, than if you just went and dug them straight up. Now wind most of the line round the top of the rod, or it will get in the way. You only want about a yard above the float, as you are going to crawl carefully to that corner and just drop the worm over the edge. I shouldn't wonder if the float went straight down, as if it was made of lead. Mind you pull at once if it does, and you'll find a perch at the other end. Now off you go very quietly, and just drop it in over the bank. Only look over just enough to see the float. There ! what did I tell you ? Went straight down, didn't it ? Don't jump and shout if you can help it, as there are some more there, waiting for another worm to drop down from the skies, and wondering where Brother Bill has gone to in that funny way. Catch hold of Brother Bill, and don't prick your fingers on those beautiful fins, and crawl back here to me. Take him off carefully—those hooks are often liable to break just where the gut joins the hook, as they may have been in the shop for a long time—and kill him and put him in the shade under that thorn bush and cover him with damp grass. A good sportsman always brings home his bag looking as nice and fresh as possible : it's no good hurrying back to those others ; they'll bite all the better if you keep them waiting for a minute. Now you may crawl back and bring another, and then one more, but I

expect that will be about all, as the others are getting a
bit lonely, and miss Sister Sally, who has just gone aloft
like poor Tom Bowling. I should work all round the
pond like that, before you do anything else, and by the
time you have done I should not wonder if you have
got nearly as many perch as we imagined last night.
And don't they make a jolly picture all together in the
cool green grass? Now we'll try to cover them up with
some beautiful silvery roach, with a little red fin. I
expect we shall find them at the lower end, where the
water begins to get shallow. I think I should take the
lead off and put the float only a yard from the hook.
I rather wish we'd brought something else besides worms,
as roach don't always like them. What they like best is
wheat boiled quite soft, and then two grains stuck on the
hook; but in a place like this, where one has to throw
out the line a bit, it is very difficult to do it without the
wheat coming off. It is not easy anyway to throw the
line with a rod like this. What you have to try to do is
to make as little splash as possible. I should take off that
heavy float and put on a long thin one, made with a piece
of quill. Swing the line out sideways, and then give it
a jerk forwards, and try to let it fall lightly on the water,
so as not to frighten them. You ought to practise on
the lawn at home, but that was not bad : now let the
water pull it towards the stream at the end, and when
you get a fish, don't haul him right out and make a great
disturbance, but bring him quietly along here under your
feet and then lift him out. Watch that float of yours
carefully. If it goes off with a jerk, it is probably only a
little fish and you won't get him, but give a little pull to
try. No: I thought you wouldn't. But he's very
likely got your worm, so pull it in quietly and look.
Little beast! On with another and here's for better
luck. That's not a bad cast. Now keep still. That's

what I like to see, a little dip down of one end of the
float. Ah! you shouldn't have pulled then; he was
only tasting to see if it was a good worm. But leave it
alone, it is not in a bad place there. There it dips again.
Keep still! And again and again and then slowly down.
Now pull, not too hard. You've got him. Bring him
along quietly, as roach are very shy fish. Never let the
line go slack, that's the only thing to be careful of. They
nearly always get off if you do. Now lift him quickly
out and kill him and put him with the perch. I don't
know which I think the prettier, but roach soon lose
their beauty when they have been out of the water a bit.
We will get two or three more, and lose a few for certain,
as they bite very light, and then we'll have lunch, to
console us for the ones which got away, especially the
fine one which wriggled off just as we were lifting him
out of the water. And before we begin again, just
remember, when you break a hook, to keep all the bits
of gut, as they will knot together, when you have got
enough, into quite a nice end for your fishing line: and
the fish won't see it so well as they'll see the other. If
you have any spare money, I should always advise you
to buy some loose gut and loose hooks from a good
shop, and tie your own hooks on with fine silk rubbed
with wax. You'll learn to do it very neatly after one or
two tries, and you may be able to get enough to make
quite a long end for your line, and mind you dry it at the
end of the day, and rub a little oil into it, and then it will
last a long time. I do like fellows to be a bit careful with
their things: it so often means that one has a lusty copper
put away somewhere, which we should not have had,
if we had been careless with our things. And I did
want one so very badly sometimes, after I had spent it
on something that I oughtn't to have wanted. And it
is just horrid asking for one, when you know how scarce
they are.

I don't think we shall do a very great deal more, between you and me : an August afternoon is a sleepy time for both men and fishes. But you will catch a few eels on the far side, where it is muddier, and perhaps that tench we talked about. There is no very great art in it. Chuck the worm in and wait, and when the eel comes wriggling out put your foot on him as soon as you can, or he will tangle your line up and make it all into a nasty slimy mess. I once saw a pike about a foot and a half long under the ash-tree, but I never could catch him. I hardly knew how, but if I had to do it now, I should splice a hook on to a piece of fine wire, like one uses to tie up flowers, and then catch a minnow or two in one of the streams, and run the hook just through the minnow's upper lip, and drop it in without a float. I expect he would go for it : he'd be sure to some day or other, and he wouldn't be able to cut the wire on his teeth as he would have cut the ordinary gut. Now we'll just have a little swim, and then set some night-lines, which is quite easy. About two yards of string and a hook tied on and a bit of lead. Then cut a pretty strong peg to fasten the line tight to, and stick the peg well into the bank just under water, and throw the line in with a good worm well on the hook. Try to hide them as much as possible, but don't forget where they are yourself. Other fellows will try to find them, just as I always made a point of looking well for any I could find. I don't quite know what the rules about finding are now, as I haven't had a chance of setting any for some time. But they used to be, " Take the fish, and put on another worm, and throw the line in again." One beast put four drowned kittens on mine once. I never made out who he was, or where he used to set his own, or I'd have got quits with him somehow, even if I'd got my own head broken in doing it. When you come to-morrow, don't pull them up and disturb

the pond till you have fished quietly round the banks.
It is one of the hardest things I know not to rush straight
to one's night-lines, but it doesn't pay really in the end.
Now we'll slope off home, when we've dressed. I love
drying in the sun and wind, with only a handkerchief to
help things on a bit. I'll tell you what we'll do on the
way, and that is, give a few of our fish to the cobbler, who
has no boys of his own to catch them for him, and besides
he gave us that lump of wax. We shall just be home in
time to clean and cook the rest of the fish for supper.

Now that gives you some idea of what I call an ordinary
sort of day at an ordinary sort of place. Of course I
was very luckily situated for that sort of thing in the
wilds of Lincolnshire, with never a hedge in it : field
divided from field by a dyke just as broad as a healthy
boy could hope to jump, without getting in (and " in "
meant mud as well as water) two out of three times ;
and about one dyke in every five only to be crossed by
pole jumping. I daresay you can hardly realise what my
out-of-door life was in that way. I can hardly remember
the day when I didn't go out, if going out meant at all
across country, as it generally did, with my jumping-pole
trailing behind me, or come home otherwise than wet
through or more or less caked with mud. And every
one of these dykes was full of fish of some sort or other,
to be caught somehow or other. You would not call
it exactly legitimate fishing, but it was none the less
charming on that account.

Before I finish this chapter I must have a bit of talk
about elementary fly-fishing, for those who have the luck
to own a fly-rod with a proper reel and everything smart
and nice. But I really think it must wait a bit longer.
Of course, it's a grand thing, and a thing that I hope
you'll all do some day. But I doubt whether I should
have ever been as keen, as I hope I am, for a day on

preserved water, with a nice rod and everything handy, if I had not learnt first all this rough and charming work in the wilds, with my own tools, and perhaps a not very exact regard for close seasons. I'm not sure whether they were invented then, and I certainly had never heard of them. I'm quite certain I should not have caught as many fish as I now expect to (I don't yet get as many as I think I deserve, or as I imagine over-night), if I had not learnt to watch the fish and their ways, what they do, what they eat, what are their hungry days, and almost what they think about, for I really believe they do think a bit, in a fishy kind of way. Nor should I certainly have kept my smart tackle as carefully as I believe I do, if I had not learnt to be economical and careful, from strict and stern necessity. I do hate, even now, to see a man with his fly-book all in a mess at the beginning of a day. There is some excuse at the end, when one has really to get a fly out in a hurry, because the fish are feeding in a hurry, and perhaps because it is just a question whether I am to catch the fish and miss the train, or miss the fish and catch the train, or catch both—

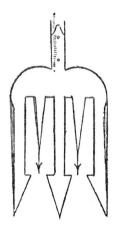

which is the greatest triumph of all. But even then, I think that the real fisherman will put his book to rights in the train, though this is more per-fection than I always, or even often, climb up to.

This smart fishing is all very nice, I say, but I don't believe that I love it as much as I loved the old rough days, when one sallied out prepared to catch fish almost anyhow, if not quite anyhow. Certainly, at one time, my jumping-pole had an eel-spear fastened on to one end—a fearsome thing

that the blacksmith made me—with which you stab
down into the mud, and sometimes over-balance and
fall in, if the mud is at all extra soft. I used to think that
the eel left a bluish spot on the mud as he went down,
but I doubt it now. Anyway I used to spear them with
some success in the dykes.

Then there were the pike up to about two pounds,
lying dozing on the weeds in these same dykes. A wire
did for them, with the help of my jumping-pole again.
You want about a yard of string, and then an ordinary
well-twisted noose of fairly strong wire tied on to the end
of it. That and a very watchful eye and steady hand are
all that are necessary, after a little practice. The only
thing to remember is that, as fish lie head up-stream, the
wire noose must come drifting down over their heads,
and not come wrong way on, from their tails, which one
is rather tempted to do, and then off they go like an arrow,
for they know that nothing comes up stream like that
without meaning mischief. So put out your pole very
slowly and steadily about six feet beyond their noses,
and let the wire noose down into the water, till it just
scrapes along the weeds, and then bring it down, about
the pace of the current to the fish. If you have calculated
badly (and it is not easy), let it brush right past them—
they don't mind it touching them—things often do—
coming that way—and then try again ; and if you see it
go nicely over their head, take it half-way, and then one
mighty heave, and oh joy! you may dance now, for
there's your first stripy-green pike, looking very vicious
and ready to bite your finger—and he will too, if you
give him a chance.

I shall never forget the day, when I caught three of
these snapping sharks ; there had been a flood, and they
had wandered inland, and got left in a pool about as big
as a small room and quite shallow, with one big roach.

I always thought that one big roach looked suspicious, as if there might have been once some smaller ones. I was rather alarmed for my toes, but pulled off my boots and went for them, and had a real happy half-hour or more.   They were very active, and so was I, and in the end I prevailed, and had all four on the grass ; the roach gave up the struggle first and weighed nearly a pound, then the big pike, just short of four, and as I caught the last of them on my hands and knees, if not rather more so, I leave you to imagine the state I was in.   But I prevailed over them all, and I can wish you nothing better than a similar half-hour of undiluted fun.   As I found a good eel walking about in the middle of a meadow, on my way home, my return was of rather a triumphant nature, and I sniffed about those meadows for many days afterwards, but got " nary 'nother."

Now just for a wee bit of fly-fishing to finish up with : I expect I'm trespassing on somebody else's ground in talking about this, but I never was very good at seeing notice boards.   I've got an excuse to make, which is the great thing, and that is that I'm not going to let you buy flies ; you've got to make your own, like a lot of the other things I've talked about.   The other fellow, who writes the other book, can talk all about the swagger article.   I'd just have given anything for someone to give me a hint or two, when I was your age, how to tie a fly good enough to catch dace and chub.   Of course, you must have a fly rod, and a proper reel and line, and a fine gut trace : I shall have to take that for granted. And to make the fly, you want patience and neatness, which both come with practice ; eyed hooks for choice, as you are by this time buying your hooks loose ; some bees-wax and fine tying silk ; a peacock's tail-feather or two, with plenty of long fine feathers from a cock's hackle, of about four colours, black, red, white and pale drab, and any more sorts you like. If you want to make wings, you will want some feathers from a young starling's wing—but these are hard to do well and you scarcely need them. Now pull one long single plume or strand out of the peacock's tail-feather, and scrape off carefully all the beautiful greeny spangle with the back of a knife. You will have left a fine substance of the nature of quill. Take this by the small end, and tie it with silk on to the hook, near the bend : about three rounds of silk will be enough. (Wax your silk well first, and then it won't slip.) Pass the silk once under itself and cut it off, leaving the least trifle over. Now take the quill by the big end, and wrap it round and round the hook, towards the head, just over-lapping every time, and taking under it the tiny end of silk, so as to fasten that in. That makes a beautiful body, with rings round it, just like a real gnat. When you get a bit more than half-way, tie it in with silk, and at the same time tie in the small end of one of the cock's feathers, and do the silk as before. Now wrap the feather round and round up to the head, and you will find it stick out beautifully all round like a fly's hackle. Then take your silk again, and fasten off the end just by the eye of the hook. You will have to invent a secure fasten-ing off for your silk this time, as there is nothing new coming on to pass it under. But you will soon manage. Just a snip or two with a pair of scissors will tidy up everything, and you will find that the fly you have made is good enough to catch fish. [The fly in the picture is made without scraping the spangle off the peacock's feather.]

You'll want big hooks and little hooks, the former for the evening and the latter for the day, and when you've once made that fly neatly in four plain colours, you will

easily find out varieties for yourself.   If you want to vary
the body, make it all of well-waxed silk, with snippings
of hare's or rabbit's or mole's fur plastered against the
greasy silk between your fore-finger and thumb.   The
wrapping round and round the hook will hold the greater
part of the snippings fast, and then you can try different-
coloured silks for the body.   So you will make quite a fine
collection of useful flies for yourself, and become so
neat-fingered at the same time, that your mother will
hardly know you, certainly not your sisters.   How to
chuck these flies on to the water is beyond my teaching.
Try to throw a whip lash out straight and light on the
lawn ; then a short line with the rod, and then a longer
line with the rod, and then go down to the river, where
the stream is pretty quick and the dace lie, and try to put
the fly lightly over them, with as long a line as you can
comfortably cast, and after that try the chub in the evening
with a big white fly.   You'll catch them soon enough :
it is all patience and perseverance, and won't you be
pleased and proud, when you have caught your first
fish on a fly of your own making !   I really believe
it is almost a happier moment than when your first
salmon lies at your feet either in Norway or bonny
Scotland.

   I have about told you all I know—don't you imagine
it is a quarter of what there is to learn.   Fishing would
be no fun if it was.   I think we all love it so dearly because
it is so full of surprises.   I doubt whether anyone will
ever know all that fish are capable of.   I was teaching a
beginner to fly-fish from a boat last year, and he kept
flicking the water behind him with his fly as he made his
casts.   A little trout spotted the game and took the fly
behind the boat and was flicked right over our heads into
the water in front, where he went off rejoicing to tell
his pals about the new game he had invented, but they

did not seem to think it good enough, for no more
tried it.

Of course I have been extraordinarily lucky all my life.
First the lovely fens of Lincolnshire, with their waving
reed-beds and countless dykes and ponds and canals,
where the fish simply hunger for the succulent worm,
and the wily eel slimes about in the mud.   Then the
banks of the Trent, with its big chub and lively dace, and
its many neighbouring ponds, where the great bream lie
beside the water-lilies, and you can see them rooting
about among the stems, while the broad leaves loll half
out of the water, as if a wind was lifting them, and the
pike lurk by the fringe of reeds or bask on the weed-beds,
with their flat ugly heads and savage eyes on the watch
for the unwary sprat.   And now last of all Winchester
and its water-meadows, much written about and loved of
many, nurse of many a boy fisherman and lover of nature,
from Frank Buckland to my young friends and celebrities
of the future, who rush about those damp and oozy
meadows, summer and winter, booted or bootless, chasing
the nimble crayfish with a butterfly net from stone to
stone in the little feeders of the main streams, till at last
they run him in up by the tiny sluice and bring him home
with his brothers and sisters to boil for tea : or casting,
many of them, as good a fly as even Sir Edward Grey,
another of the band, could wish to see, where the big
trout still suck in the " olives " under the far bank, as I
have no doubt they did in his day : or even, I fear, sneak-
ing down with their worm or with their minnow to the
deep pool below Gunner's Hole, thence to extract a
breakfast for themselves or a conciliatory present for their
" Div. Don," lest he should bear too hardly those half-
prepared Cæsar lessons, which are the natural and reasonable consequence.   O those summer days, with the
spotty and stripy and shiny fishes !   Who that has ever

enjoyed them would not risk the wrath even of the immortals, and shirk all sorts of serious business, to steal forth to the water? Who would not? Ay, and who does not? Kids, I ask it of you? Young men, what of you? Greybeards? Why! I do it myself.

CHAPTER II

BIRDS AND THEIR NESTS

I WONDER if there exists such a thing as a boy who has never bird-nested. The very fact of the common occurrence, though you probably won't find it in a dictionary, of the verb "to bird-nest" seems to prove how widespread is the practice. And yet it is mostly forbidden by law, and rightly, and our rarer birds are becoming more plentiful, in Hampshire at any rate, in consequence. And more power to the elbow of the law, say I, as I care more now for the birds than for their eggs, being rather short in the wind for climbing; nor do I greatly care now to scratch my hands and person generally in hedges and gorse bushes. But O my! how I loved it once, and how I love it still, if the truth will out. I have learnt a sort of forbearance with age, and can look at a nest of eggs without taking any—I was just going to write "without wanting to," but that would not have been true. I always want to pick the best specimen, and sneak home, and drill a neat hole in the side, and blow with a blow-pipe, and wash it out well with water, and stand it for an hour on blotting paper, and then, joy of joys, add it to the much-loved collection, and if it should be the first of its kind, and have a compartment all to itself, what pride and exultation. Only two years ago, I made my first acquaintance with the ringed plover in this way, and went through the whole process, and came to the conclusion that I was just as young as when I got my first hedge-sparrow's egg—well! never you mind how many years ago. Nor do I think I will tell you all just where it was. You shall find your own place, at the end of April, and not go and bully my little friends in Somewhereshire. There was, and is still I suppose, a small low-lying island in an estuary. If you don't know what that is, seek in a geography. It was mostly mud-banks when I was there, but there were two or three long spits of gravel, and on these the eggs were laid. I can find the eggs of the lapwing and stone-curlew, but these are certainly harder. Like all other nests, it is the first that is the hardest. When your eye once learns what it is expected to see, it very soon proves itself a reasonably useful organ. At least, I have no complaints to make of mine, though the books say that a tomtit has a better one than I have. The birds scrape a little hollow among the pebbles, but where the pebbles are big, I am sure that they only take a convenient arrangement of big pebbles, and fill in the cracks and corners a bit. I found some eggs that looked simply to have been laid among the stones, until I lifted them up, when I found such a small nest as I have described, with the uncomfortable places just smoothed off, and decorated, just like an oystercatcher does, with bits of broken shell. I expect it was all right as a nest, but, as far as catching your eye went, it was no use at all.   You just saw a lot of stones and four eggs uncommonly like them.

I should think I could have got twenty nests on that little island, and the oyster-catchers were just beginning to scrape and decorate their hollows, while the sheldrakes on the mainland were investigating the rabbit-holes with a view to setting up housekeeping, and quarrelling with the landlady as to terms, and one pair of redshanks had found a decent tuft of grass in which to lay their pretty pear-shaped eggs.   And a little farther along the coast there was a bit of marshland, where I saw certainly ten lapwings' nests, full of eggs, nearly ready to hatch by that time, I expect.   And I thought to myself how many of my acquaintances I could take over that island and along that bit of coast, who would never have the smallest idea that there was an egg within miles of them, and realised that there was a great deal of extra pleasure to be got out of life by a little knowledge of birds and their lives and ways.

But I am afraid that, in sketching briefly a little scene, which stands out very clearly before my eyes, I may have made some of you ardent egg-collectors gnash your teeth, for it is not given to everyone to find in the same day eggs of the ringed plover, lapwing, and red-shank, with promise of those of the oyster-catcher and sheldrake.   Some of you may never even have found a lapwing's nest for yourselves, and yet it is not difficult, as there is really a certain amount of nest.   In the Midlands they frequent the fields of young corn, and I found my first nest by going laboriously from side to side down each furrow.   Now, of course, I should just hide myself in the hedge, and watch the birds through a field-glass : but I used to find that, if you approached each hedge very carefully, and showed yourself suddenly, the bird rose off the nest without running and you could walk straight up to it. Later on, when the tiny young ones are about, the old birds get extraordinarily bold, if you are anywhere near their precious family, swooping down with wild screams close past your head ; but if you can see a young lapwing squatting on a bare road, you have no need to complain of your eyesight.

What exploit in the bird-nesting line will you look back upon with the greatest pride, when you are my age ? I think that one of my heron's eggs gives me more satisfaction than any other egg in my collection, partly because I got it out of such very sacred precincts, that even after the lapse of nearly twenty years, I dare not tell you where it was laid, though the scene was one of extraordinary beauty, and I should love to describe it. I feel sure, if I were to lift the veil, that I should be run in for high treason, or something of the kind, and be drawn and quartered, or burnt alive, before I quite knew where I was : partly also because it was the last good climb I ever did, and perhaps the biggest I ever did. I was always a good climber, owing I suppose to length of leg and arm. I never used irons or any artificial help, but hugged the trunk and went up. My shins were always a picture in May. And for this particular egg, I had a climb of some twenty feet, without anything like a branch, to start on, and that sort of thing at four o'clock on a March morning is no joke. I thought I should never reach branches, but I did at last, and finally got to the nest, very blown and rather scared, partly because of the height, which was beyond my experience, and partly because of two very irate old herons, who were swooping about, making weird noises in their throats ; but they spared me, to my great relief. They had me on toast, if they had really gone for me. I found two young birds, one egg with the kid's head out, and another with the shell unbroken. This latter, when I got safely down,

I put into cold water, for fear it should hatch in my pocket,
and in the end I got a beautiful specimen, thanks to a
fine pair of tweezers and a little pair of surgical scissors,
which someone stole not long afterwards. Ill may they
prosper the thief.   You couldn't call the egg blown.
It was a case of accurate carving, such as you can do with
a big strong-shelled egg, not with a small one ; so never
be tempted to take a small egg, unless it is pretty fresh ;
it is mere waste of life.   And when you take a large one,
gum over the part where you are going to drill the hole
a square of brown paper, and let the gum harden.   Then
drill the hole right through the paper.   This will prevent
the sides of the hole from chipping, when you are pulling
at and carving a piece of the bird inside.   When all is
done, fill the egg with water, and let it stand for a night,
to get out the inside skin which has veins of blood in it
and will decay and spoil the specimen, if allowed to stay
there.   Then wash off the square of brown paper, and
dry the egg carefully on blotting-paper, and you ought
to have as good a specimen as if it had been fresh.

So much for a successful expedition after a pretty
good egg.   Now for a failure.   Only two years ago I
was in Cornwall, fishing on Bodmin Moor.   My last
whole day was too windy to allow me to fish with any
pleasure, so I went to look for some ravens that I had
seen about, and got so near to getting them, as to put
the old bird off the nest, some thirty feet above my head,
but no nearer could I get.   You may be sure that I tried
all I knew, short of breaking my neck, but I do not think
that, in the palmiest days of my climbing, I could have
got at that nest.   Mr. Williams has drawn me a beautiful
picture of the place, so that you can get some idea how
tantalising a nest can be.   The only thing about it is,
that I have got him to make the cleft in the rock, and
the nest itself, about three sizes too big, for the sake of

clearness. It seemed to me that there were four ways of
getting at the nest, all of which were prevented by some
tiresome misfortune. One was to climb on to the top
of the rock, and get down from there, by the help of a
rope. I got with some difficulty and uneasiness on to
the top of the rock, but the face had a big bulge directly
below me, which meant that a rope would have swung

ten feet away from the nest. Of course, if I had had time,
I could have let myself swing there, and fished the eggs
out with a bag on the end of my rod. That was the
only possible way that I could see. Another way was to
climb along a rather nasty crack on the left of the picture
on to the top (and a very sloping top too) of the big

rock jutting out from the main rock, and use my rod
from there. I got there, again with much anxiety, and
found that, owing to an angle in the rock, I could not
even see the nest. I then scrambled up to the fissure
itself, and tried to climb this by pressing my back against
one side and putting my feet against the other, but it
got too narrow, and even if I could have climbed higher,
I could never have got my hands round the stone, which
was jammed at the top, and on which the nest was built.
Lastly the nest was within reach of a good ordinary ladder,
but the ground fell away so steep at the bottom of the
fissure, that it would have taken an hour's careful digging
to make any sort of foothold for the bottom of the ladder,
let alone the fact that I should have had to bring the
ladder a very rough three miles. I can't call the nest
really inaccessible, given time and a man to help. But
under the circumstances it was too much for me, and I
gave it up. I was not altogether disappointed with the
expedition. I barked my shins all over, and scratched
my hands finely, which was a pleasing reminiscence of
boyhood. And I had a very good look at the ravens,
who resented my presence, and came very close to me,
croaking and making the most interesting noises, so that
their throats under their beaks puffed out enormously,
and their splendid plumage was almost blue in the bright
sunshine. Jolly old beggars ! Long may they live to
breed in that fissure, and may everyone who finds out
their whereabouts enjoy their rock-climbing as much as
I did, and meet with no better success. It would vex me
enormously to hear that anyone had just strolled up to
that nest and got a raven's egg.

Since I began to write this chapter, I have had a great
responsibility put upon me, but one that promises much
enjoyment, if all turns out well. A pair of lesser spotted
woodpeckers have chosen my garden, on the outer suburbs

of Winchester, as their breeding-place. They began to
dig on Saturday, May 11, and scattered chips all over my
lawn and walk, as if there had been a wooden snowstorm.
On Sunday they were out of sight inside the tree, but
you could hear them hammering thirty yards away. I sat
and watched them with a pair of glasses. I say them,
but I never saw more than one at work. His head
appeared at the entrance to the hole, about once every
half-minute, with a bit of wood, which he flicked away
with a shake of his head, and then dived down for another.
After a while, about half-an-hour, he came out and sur-
veyed his work from outside, and then flew off. In about
five minutes, presumably the other bird came, and did
her share of the work. This went on till Tuesday mid-
day, when they disappeared, and I have not seen them
since. I have no doubt things are going on well, and
that there are now three eggs in the nest, for they have
never been disturbed in the least, which speaks well for
a house of three dozen boys, and even for a bird-nesting
master, who have none of them ever seen the egg of a
lesser spotted woodpecker. I don't think any outsider
will get those eggs ; we want them ourselves too much
to let anyone else take what we have spared, and the tree
is not a very easy one, considering that there would be
an hour's chopping at the top of it, before the nest could
be reached. So I have hopes that we shall yet see those
young ones crawling about the trunk, and being fed by
their spotted parents, which ought to be a very pretty
sight, and one not given to everybody to see. But, as
I say, it is an anxiety, and I sleep with my bedroom window
very wide open, and the nest is not fifteen yards away.
I think of it so much, that I am sure I should wake if
anyone tried to take it at night, and then there would be
the rousing of a hornet's nest, and I pity the would-be
thief. How I should have enjoyed scheming to get it,

in early days, out of someone else's garden! Well—
set a thief to catch a thief. I have great hopes of seeing
those young ones, but am afraid I shall not be able to
tell you about them, as time is getting on, and I have
lots still to write about, and none too much time for
writing, in this gorgeous summer weather. However, I'll
try to get in a note[1] at the bottom of the page, to say
whether all went well. The picture[2] shows you the tree,
with Mike and Tiddles cat-hunting—but not very seriously,
as it is their own cat. The birds had not come when
this was taken. The nest is right at the top of the right
hand branch, which was cut off short last year about ten
feet above the cat.

The woodcock is another bird I have seen a good
deal of at Lyndhurst in the New Forest, and whose eggs
I have never touched, though sorely tempted. I think
it was really, to speak quite frankly, not so much a desire
to spare the feelings of Mr. Lascelles, or to uphold the
reputation of his excellent keepers and watchers (and
really excellent they are), as the feeling that, if I resisted
the temptation, there would be another woodcock for
someone to shoot or shoot at. Perhaps on the whole,
it was general love of the bird, whose big eye watched
me so quietly and unflinchingly, as she sat cuddled up
there among the dead bracken and beech leaves. They
really ought to shut those eyes; I should never have
seen her, but for her eye. I had to put her off quietly
to look at the eggs, but she was back all right in a quarter
of an hour. People have written a great deal as to the

[1] I never saw the birds till the young ones hatched. Then they
came and went very stealthily every quarter of an hour, until the
young ones were able to feed at the mouth of the hole. But I never
saw them outside. They were carried off, I suppose, to the bigger
trees in the park across the road.

[2] See Frontispiece.

way in which they carry their young. There may be many ways, but I am sure of one, for I could have twice touched them with my stick. The first time, Master Woodcock fancied his own flying powers, but his Ma wouldn't let him try. She swooped on him, and knocked him down, and plainly and visibly tried to clutch him, neither with beak nor feet, but with her wing, and he wriggled out, and had another indignant try for himself, and was again knocked down, and the whole process was repeated. I kept close up and watched it all. Some years afterwards I disturbed quite a tiny one, and the mother again came and took it under her wing and flew off with it, almost from under my feet, and I saw its head peep out where her wing joins her body. She flew badly. So I can only suppose that she managed to use the wing enough to fly, and little enough to clutch the kid with the feathers at the base of the wing. It doesn't sound a very easy task. I can only describe what I saw at very close quarters ; and I watched most carefully, knowing that the question was much discussed. It was a charmingly pretty sight, on both occasions, as well as an absorbingly interesting one. And I have seen another, which I shall never forget, though I did not know at the time that it was under dispute—and that was an adder opening her mouth, and all her kiddies bolting in. It was quite fifteen years ago, and I had never heard of such a thing happening. So I only made a vivid mental note of the fact, and let her slip away. Now that people have asserted the fact so violently, and denied the possibility so violently, I suppose it is your duty to kill her, and tie up her throat, and send her up to the British Museum to be investigated. But whether she has anywhere to put them or not, I have seen them disappear into her mouth, if I can trust my eyes at all, and I could still take you to the square foot of ground on which I saw her, I believe. That's nothing

to do with birds, but the woodcock question reminded
me of it, and it may interest you.   Keep a watch for it
yourselves, and if you see it, join your voice to mine and
others somehow.

I wonder, to talk of other queer things in Bird Life,
how young wild ducks get down from some of the strange
places in which a thoughtless parent sees fit to hatch
them.   They must have a very interesting and adventurous
infancy.   I have never managed to be present at any of
these household removals, though in one particular case,
at any rate, I tried very hard to hit off the time.   The
birds breed pretty freely among the long grass and sedges
of our water-meadows, but owing to the presence of so
many marauding young ruffians, I suppose, don't find it
a very paying game, and are driven to strange shifts.
Twice I have found a nest on the top of the downs, among
some scrubby heather, a good mile away from water.
That only gave the brood a longish walk to the river,
which I daresay came off all right, with perhaps the loss
of one or two, who went to the larder of one of the many
weasels that live thereabouts.   Another nest was on the
top of a straw-stack, also a good mile off the river ; so
that they had a nice drop, as well as a long walk. I found
no corpses, but the rats may have had cold duckling,
if the fall killed any.   The most fascinating nest of all
was half-way up a big elm tree, where a large branch
joined the trunk and made a nice hollow.   I saw the bird's
beak, and thought ' That looks like a duck's beak ' ; and
when I tapped the trunk, off she went.   I saw her often,
and eventually found the shells under the tree, but I
would like to have seen her bring her family down, and
wasted hours watching.   The river was only thirty yards
off, but too far for them to tumble into it.   I daresay a
young duck is rather like india-rubber, and a fall on the
soft grass does not hurt it.   But whether the Spartan

mother pushes them off, or whether they come down on her back, or in her beak, or under her wing like the woodcock, I can't say. Most people seem to fancy that they are pushed out. Anyway it's a cheery start in life to take a drop of thirty feet, and no wonder that duck become the wary, shifty fowl that those who pursue the fascinating sport of shooting them find them to be. Different people swear by different notes of birds, as the most delightful; and I am not sure whether I don't like as well as any other the distant quack in the half-light of a December evening, which warns you that you will soon hear the swish of wings, and get the shot for which you have waited so long and patiently, while the sunlight fades off the water, and all the world grows dim and grey, and, from your point of view, full of the expectancy now about to be realised. But you must hold straight, and follow on quick with your swing, or there will be no dull thud or splash to follow the spurt of flame into the darkness. And you must keep most uncommonly quiet all the time, or they will swerve past you out of shot and out of sight. It was not for nothing that they began a life of adventures adventurously.

For a long time I made rather a special study of my rascally old friend, the carrion crow, and I'm afraid he's a rascal, but, like many another rascal, an uncommonly attractive old bird. To begin with, he's a coarse feeder, and prefers garbage to clean meat; and I fancy he's often accused of killing a game-bird, which some clumsy shot has sent away to die, and which he has found and appropriated. I know that, if I could meditate such an act of treachery towards an old friend as baiting a trap for him, I should employ a bird or rat that had seen better days, and that, if no longer alive in the proper sense of the word, was very much alive in another. He's a foolhardy old scamp, too, in the way of his nest, building

D

where everyone can see it, which very fact suggests to my mind that, if he is not innocent of crime from our point of view, he is entirely unconscious in his own heart of any but the highest motives, and I feel sure that, when he is greeted with a cartridge, as he so often is, he dies protesting against the wickedness of a world which will insist on misinterpreting the most blameless action. Sweet old ruffian! it is a joy to hear him cawing good-night from a tree-top, in a voice made hoarse by much high feeding. I had a merry time getting my first eggs in the old Lincolnshire days, for my pole broke in jumping an intervening dyke, and I had to do a rather serious climb dripping wet, and plastered with mud, and my boots kept slipping on the branches. My last visit to his home was just the opposite, during the same visit to Cornwall in which I was mocked by the ravens. I was fishing with some success in the River Camel, when I saw a nest in a small oak tree in a hedge, and a stone among the branches put off the hen. It was so obviously easy, that I walked up to it in my waders, and had a look at the four green eggs in their soft lining of wool. Could any bird build a conspicuous great nest, in a tree that a heavy man in waders could walk up, unless it was firmly convinced that its general life was so blameless, that active and malignant enemies were out of the question? It's dead against all the laws of Natural Selection. Therefore I say, love and spare the carrion crow.

This is a great county for birds, but they have been so much written about, and so charmingly, that I find it very difficult to write about them at all in my turn. But you might like to know what sort of a bird-nesting walk I could take you here. In the early spring, we could go up into the downs, where I would guarantee to show you eggs of the lapwing, very likely on the top of an old molehill; then we would drop down to a plantation of

spruce firs in one of the hollows, haunted by a very stern
and savage keeper, who has no taste for the sight of
silver, more credit to him.   But he need not catch us,
unless his dog is with him.   You young folks go about
preserves singing and talking and laughing and walking
on dead sticks.   You have no taste for silence.   But an
old man like me creeps in quietly, and then sits down
and listens.   What I want to hear is the song of the
goldcrest, a little tiny song in a tiny voice, but never to
be mistaken for anything else, when once you know it.
Then I will creep from bush to bush in the undergrowth,
and watch for the birds, and when I have found them
the nest is easy ; you will probably be able to see it on
the under-side of one of the long sweeping boughs of
the tree in which the birds are, about six feet from the
ground.   If not there, it is in another tree very near,
with its tiny buffish-orange tinged eggs in their cosy
cradle of moss.   Listen a moment, and if you don't hear
the keeper, you will have time to look at it, for very few
keepers walk *quite* noiselessly, though they are a quiet
race.   Then hide again, and creep warily out, and we will
go down to the river-side.   There is gorse on the slopes
of the down facing the river, and a couple of stonechats
are flickering about.   They seem to know that you have
read that they often nest at the foot of a gorse bush, and
so they dance from one to the other, standing on tip-toe
with fluttering wings on the prickly tips of the gorse,
one calling " Here you are ! " whilst the other bobs up
and cries " This bush for stonechat's eggs ! "   And so
you'll get fooled about from one to the other, if you
believe them.   I daresay the books are right enough,
but I've never found their nest anywhere but in a bank,
just like a robin's.   So if you'll disregard their antics,
and come down to the river bank, I'll show you the nest
tucked away in the long grass : and I could take you to

three more similar bits of gorse country, where the birds
are a good fifty yards away from their nest in the bank of
a little grass lane, popping about in the gorse, and trying
to get you to scratch your legs and lose your temper.
They are nearly the earliest breeders here, though the
long-tailed tit runs them close. I wonder why so many
novelists, who want to make the whole world kin with a
touch of nature, pick this bird's nest to unite the hero and
heroine over, generally in July, if not later. Having
viewed these pretty pale blue eggs with their brown
speckles, we'll set off on a good three-mile tramp to the
pond where the coots breed. You can see their nests
about five or ten yards from the bank among the bul-
rushes. But here again is a very wary keeper, so either
you or I must go and sing songs in his preserves, and
lure him away, like Ariel, from his pond, but he can
run more than a little, so you'll want all your wind, or
he'll have you. He'll try all he knows, and will run
exactly as long as his wind holds out, which is as well
for you, as he has a fine command of language, when he
has any breath left to form the words. The other of us
will take an egg or two, for they can well be spared, but
mind you tread on the tufts of rushes or you'll sink in
the mud above your knees, and may get caught after all,
in which case you'll suffer. We'd better arrange to meet
at Winchester, for you will have to run a good bit of the
way there, if you are to shake off your determined pursuer :
and that will about finish off an average sort of day in the
early part of the season. If you elect to come out with
me later on, I shall have much more difficulty in knowing
what to do. There are kingfishers, thanks to the laws,
now becoming much commoner in the banks of the
river and its many tributaries, in the water-meadows.
You can pretty generally find their nests by smelling at
the various rat-holes, if your nose is at all in reasonable

working order. Of course, now and then, you will dig out a dead rat, but you ought to learn to distinguish so comparatively mild a perfume as that from the much more vicious one of putrefying fish-bones. They are not all fish-bones by any means, for a considerable selection is made from the various dead cats and dogs which adorn our placid stream, as they do most others, I suppose, from time to time. They are very careful birds in the way they approach their nest : I knew of one pair who had their nest in our boys' bathing-place. You'd think there were sharp enough eyes there to detect so rash an attempt, and I am afraid that they were eventually discovered, but only by a young gentleman, who had concealed himself there—well ! if the truth must out—to smoke the forbidden and pernicious cigarette. The birds, I suppose, thought the place empty and got a bit careless. Of course, when the young ones come, they get quite reckless, and fly in and out with fish at very short intervals. To go to rarer birds still, I have often heard the grasshopper warblers, like a big locust, in the hedge-bottoms, and found their nest once low down among the tangle that had grown up round the roots, but it was rather a fluke, and there were only young ones in it. I was glad on the whole to be spared the temptation of eggs. Does it sound strange to you to hear a man talking of being glad that he missed a chance of rare eggs ? I assure you it's true, and you'll come to the time yourself, little as you believe it now. I can't say that I ever expect a boy to refuse a good egg when luck puts it in his way : all I would take the opportunity to say is " Be sparing." One rare egg out of one nest, even if you never get another, is to my mind a far greater ornament to a boy's collection than five that have obviously come out of the same nest. People nowadays talk a lot of nonsense about the scientific value of a whole clutch.

Of course there is plenty of scientific value in a way, but not one man in fifty either to appreciate it or make any use of it. What truth of nature does the fact that one clutch of wren's eggs has more markings than another impress upon an ordinary collector's mind ? It seems to me all a bit of self-deception that we have got into, either to cloak our greed, which cannot spare half a nest at any rate, or else to foster a fond belief that we shall all be Darwins in time, if we stick to wholesale robbery long enough. There ! That's a bit of my mind, and don't you forget it. And don't say, " If I don't have them, someone else will." It may be true enough, but I can't see that it makes your position any better. But let's go back to our birds, and I'll set you a really difficult task—so difficult that I have not managed to accomplish it myself yet, and never shall now, I suppose. That is, find me the nest of the water-rails. I know they always breed in a particular osier bed down the river-side, for I have watched them for hours, poking about among the sedges, with my field-glass ; but, as far as their movements go, their nest might be anywhere. I suppose there are two pairs really, and that the two restless creatures, who are playing hide-and-seek in the sedges, are the two gentlemen, waiting for the family to be hatched by their ladies at home, and having a real good holiday before their domestic worries begin, but I wish it would occur to them to go and take a turn at sitting on the eggs some-times, and then I might learn the whereabouts of the nest. It is rather vexatious being beaten by a bird, but you may hunt those sedges for hours and get no forrader. The other birds that defeated my best efforts for a long time were the wheatears. There were only two pairs about, as far as I could make out, and each in a small colony of rabbits. Of course, I could not dig out ten rabbit-holes one day, and then ten the next ; the owners might have come and asked for explanations with a stick. So I thought I'd be surpassingly cunning, and one day I toiled off with a big bag of dry sand, amid the jeers of the populace, and sprinkled a nice layer in the mouth of each of the holes, thinking to find, by the footprints, which was the hole into which the wheatears went (sounds rather like " Which was the peck of pickled peppers that Peter Piper's peacock picked "). But they weren't to be done that way. I went full of hope next day, and found that they had been down every single hole, or else they thought I had put the sand for them to dance on. I was cross, I tell you ; and I threw many flints at those flickering white tails. (I wonder, by the way, whether wheatears and rabbits live together because they both have white tails, and, if so, why the bullfinches have been left out.) But my right hand had lost its cunning, and I did no harm. It relieved my feelings, however, and showed the deceitful little beasts what I thought of them. Their treachery was even greater than I imagined, for I found the nest, when there were young ones in it, beside a big stone, right away from the rabbit-holes. I have found them since those days in rabbit-holes, but never very far down.

Don't you love swifts ? I really think, if I had to be a bird, I'd be a swift. I believe I'd win a lot of races, obstacle races at any rate. The way in which they fly full tilt at a wall, and then just flick to one side with those long narrow wings, is amazing, and must be rare fun for them. And how they squeal with joy, about a dozen of them, as they race round and round, and in and out, and then tower straight up, and come swooping down again.

It's a funny thing, but all the members of the swallow and martin family have such very quiet voices. The sand martin only seems to say ' Yes ' and ' No,' as it flutters over the water, and even then you can hardly hear it. The house martin gossips away very prettily to his wife, as they cling to the wall and discuss which is the best place for the first dab of mud ; and I have even heard them use rather strong language when the rascally sparrows tried to turn them out of their houses, which had taken so long to build, and generally succeeded too. Beasts ! How angry I got when my poor little pair of white-stockinged martins had to begin all over again. And the swallow has really got quite a song, which he sings, sitting on a bough, like any other bird ; and a very pretty cry of alarm and consternation, when he finds you too near his nest. It makes me think of an old cow-shed in Lincolnshire, where I killed my first rat with a fire-shovel, in rather a funk lest he should get the better of me. I had read awful stories of the danger of getting a rat with his back to the wall, and how he ran up your legs, and had you by the throat. I got him in just such a tight corner and smote him, so he had no chance of trying my throat. I used to hide behind the door, and when the swallows flew in, slam the door, and catch them on the old cobwebby window, and then let them go again. They couldn't have minded it much, because they finished their nest and got off their young. But it strikes me now as rather brave of them, and the alarm cry always reminds me how they gave one agonised shout, when they found that the nasty door had gone and shut itself again, and another, as they flew away from my open hand some five minutes afterwards. But the cheery old swifts have no modesty when they are asked for a song. Songs with a good chorus are what they like, and don't they join in lustily ! Rather out of tune, as far as I can make out, but a real good chorus for all that. Like Winchester men, singing ' Domum.' And a pretty safe ' domum ' it is, too ; generally tucked away with its .

badly shaped eggs in a place beyond the reach of boy's fingers. I've a pair now in the wall of my fives-court, and they have great quarrels when they are feeding the kids and both arrive with a fly at the same time. I have seen them come slithering down the wall, biting and scratching, till they were within a foot of the ground (Tiddles, the dog who climbs trees, only just missed them once), and then off they went for more flies, to replace those that had been lost in the scuffle. Jolly black imps ! they do enjoy life. Make me into a swift, when life becomes too dull to go on living as a man.

We are proud possessors, about two miles out of Winchester, of a smelly thing called a Sewage Farm, which brings the gulls up in clouds, in the winter— mostly common gulls and black-headed gulls. And very hard they are to distinguish in the winter, as the latter lose their black heads, when the breeding season is over. The only distinction that I can find is, that the common gull has green feet and the other one pink feet. But when you want one good specimen for a museum, out of the hundreds that come within shot, it is rather difficult not to waste life. I want a mature specimen of the common gull, and have twice taken my gun and come back without shooting anything. What I should like to do is to say " Show your feet," and then tell the possessors of green feet to toss " odd man out," for a victim. I suppose this winter I shall have to harden my heart and shoot. I'm sure to get one out of six with green legs. When I require a victim in my house for any small crime, I demand one ; then they all put twopence into the pool, and draw lots, and the man on whom the lot falls takes the coppers, faces my wrath, and goes and consoles himself with ices. I don't mention it as a good principle : but they have adopted it, and I don't find it an easy scheme to defeat. And I wish my gulls would hit upon some

similar device.   Only the ices would have to go to the
next of kin, unless I made a very bad shot.

I have never had much of the "broken wing" game
played upon me by birds : I should like to have seen
more of it.   A partridge did it once for me very prettily,
and I followed her to her heart's content over three-
quarters of a field.   She enjoyed it hugely, and so did
I, and when she finally reached the hedge, and flew off
with a derisive cackle, I think I was just as pleased at
having seen so clever a piece of acting, as she was at
having drawn me away from her family.   And on another
occasion, a tree-pipit fluttered out of a low bank, almost
under my foot, and shambled along in the dry ditch,
with a dainty little wing trailing along the ground, so
full of sorrow and anxiety, that I had to humour her, and
go down into the ditch, and try to catch her.   Of course
I had to go very slowly, or I should have compelled her
to fly too soon.   Lapwings are the birds that generally
are quoted as clever performers in this way, but they
have never shown off to me, though I have given them
every opportunity, even picking up their kids, when I
could contrive to see them.

I have said very little about bird-music, not from want
of appreciation, but from the enormous difficulty of
making its subtle charm obvious to those who have not
felt its power for themselves.   Every bird's note has its
own special flavour, and seems to me to help more than
anything else to define the owner's character ;   whether
it be the vulgar chatter of the plebeian little sparrow, or
the humble little ditty of the retiring hedge-sparrow, or
the senseless scream of the dandy jay, who knows that
his clothes are of the smartest and fit him to a nicety.
Of the more elaborate songsters, I suppose one mustn't
say that the nightingale is over-estimated, because everyone would give it the first prize, but considering how it

monopolises the praise of poets (just because it sings in the moonlight), I don't think that it beats several others by enough : neither the thrush for variety, nor the mellow blackbird for richness of tone, nor the robin amid the mists of autumn for daintiness of elocution. I ought not perhaps to bring in the missel thrush, for he has very few notes. But I never hear a certain song of Maud Valérie White's about the coming of Spring, without thinking of my big spotty old friend (who flew into my youthful face once because I dared to look into his nest) shouting out his wild melody amid the winds of March on the top of some elm or oak. And I don't know whether the fact is more creditable to the composer of the song or the bird.

And so fare ye well, my feathered friends, and if in any way I have been allowed to increase the love of you in the world which uses you none too well, considering all it owes you, I have my reward for what has been no toil to head or hand, but only a joy.

CHAPTER III

BUTTERFLIES FOR BOYS

I'M not, for the present, going to tell you a great many stories, but mean to give you a dose of pretty stiff instruction, for nothing gives the idea so much of wasted life, of a pretty, fluttering, very short life, cut off and spoiled, ruined and cast aside, and all for nothing, as a badly set-up butterfly. I sometimes, when I see such things, long to crush them to powder, because a butterfly never looks dead, and just as a drawer of really well-set specimens almost does away with the idea of death, and makes one grateful to the man who has made the pretty short-lived things happy and immortal, so a badly set specimen makes me feel as if some brute had caught and crippled the poor thing, and left it to drag itself along in pain and misery, till the mites came and mercifully made an end of it.

Therefore, all my young bug-hunting friends, lend me your longest ears. I'll try to tell you nothing but what

I regard as absolutely necessary. So perpend. First and very much foremost, you must spend a little money. This is so contrary to my usual stingy advice, that perhaps you'll realise that I mean it. Get it honestly, if you can. If not, you must go begging, beastly though it is to beg. Simply beastly, there's no other word. I can't let you have less than five setting boards. I know anxious Aunts will say that I'm like the Irishman, making one hole for the cat, and a smaller hole for the kitten, that a board that will hold a purple emperor will much more hold a purple hairstreak, but it isn't true. I'll apologise if you wish it. But again, it isn't true. And I'll explain presently. You must have five boards *or more*, or you'll produce hideous cripples. You may make them, if you want to be economical, and if you are good at carpentering. Slabs of cork are cheap. But I'm not going to tell you how; it would take too long. Buy *one*, and then make the others like it, only different sizes. And when you've got them, keep them clean. When the nice new paper gets all full of pinholes, and rough and horrid, sandpaper the whole lot off with rough sandpaper and then either repaper them, or far better, polish them off with fine sandpaper. Cork rubbed with fine sandpaper will give you a surface so smooth and soft, that it is a real joy to touch it, and you can imagine the butterfly resting his wings on it and saying " Well, this is nice and thoughtful ! "

Having settled your setting boards, it is very hard to know what is the proper beginning. I expect we'd better go out and catch a butterfly, and then do carefully everything that has to be done, until it is ready to go into the collection. So come along and don't get bored, for it is all very important.

The ordinary net you buy is good enough, but of course you can make your own cheaper : only you must buy

the tin fork : and you ought always to have a spare one
in your pocket, as they often break. The muslin bag
should be well soaked and dried to get the stiffness out
of it.   The stick should be light, and not more than a
yard long.   Most boys have far too long a stick, or far
too heavy a one.   If you try both, I think that you'll
catch most with my sort.   Now what sort of butterfly
shall we catch ? a purple emperor is too good to practise
on, and a blue too small.   I don't think we can do better
than a brimstone butterfly.   Net him carefully, and either
put him in a pill-box alive (he will sit quite quiet), or pinch
him carefully under the wings in the net.   This way will
not kill moths, remember.   And hold your pinch for a
second, for if you take your fingers away, he may turn
inside out.   And if he does turn inside out, and the
blues are always doing this, first wipe your hand dry,
then lay him in the palm of your hand, and stick a pin
through his legs, as if you were going to set him wrong
way on, and then pick him up on the pin, and blow his
wings over his back, or if they won't go that way, take a
blade of grass, and force them carefully back.   If one
side goes, the other goes too.   Then pin him sideways in
under one wing, and out under the other, and stick him
in a collecting box.   You ought to have a tin one, so
that you can keep the cork damp.   Otherwise, if you are
out all day, your butterflies will get stiff, and nothing is
so hopeless to set as a stiff butterfly.   As it is very difficult
to relax them properly, when once they have got stiff, I
should throw them away, rather than try to set them,
unless they are really rare ones.   It sounds a waste of
life and it is.   So be careful not to let them get stiff, only

don't let your care take the form of only half-killing them,
which is a way of meeting the difficulty adopted by some
people in the world.   I always think a good stick, well
applied where nature meant it, the right remedy for this

class of wickedness. And this is not the mere itching of a master's fingers, but a good solid wish. A pocket full of pill-boxes, or a good zinc collecting box, are the only proper ways to bring home your specimens in good condition. If you use the former, and don't know how to kill your butterflies at home, the best way is to bruise well with a hammer a lot of common laurel leaves, and fill a wide-mouthed jar half full, and then just open a chink of your boxes, and put two or three at a time among the leaves for a minute or two. You will find your butterflies apparently dead, but they are not really, only stupefied. You can leave them in an hour, but then they will be stiff, as well as dead. About thirty hours will unstiffen them, but this is a long time to wait, and the best thing is to pinch the butterflies, and for the moths to buy a penny-worth of oxalic acid, and keep a little bottle of it melted in water. Fill the bottle a quarter full of the powder, and then nearly to the top with water, and dip a pen-nib into this, and stab the moth among its legs, deep in, holding the pen still for a bit to let the acid sink well in, and in the case of big moths like drinkers, giving them quite three nibs full. They will never come to life again after this.

Now that we have got our specimen nicely killed, we can proceed to the more difficult business of setting, and the first thing is to pick the right board. The actual width does not much matter, as long as it is wide enough. For if the wings stick out over the edge, they will curl at the tips. It is the groove that matters. You must have a groove deep enough and wide enough, and not *too* deep or wide. This is why rather a lot of boards are a necessity. If the specimen is to be a nice one, the wings must rest on the cork from *very near* the base to the tip. The next thing is the pins : most boys use far too large ones. I can't stand a poor little blue impaled

on a thing that one could well have used to spear an eel.
Most boys' collections took more like a pin forest than a
box of butterflies.   You want one no longer than the
body of the butterfly, from head to tail, and these fine
small pins are expensive, so be careful of them and don't
litter them about.   Now we come to the most necessary
thing of all, and the most difficult : the whole success of
the specimen depends on it ; and that is to put the pin
in straight.   That is to say, it must go into the body
exactly between the wings, and *come out* exactly between
the wings.   One can generally put it in right, but it so
often comes out nearer one wing than the other, and this
makes the whole body and wings sit crooked on the
board.   It is not a bad thing to put the pin with its head
pointing a trifle forward : that is, coming out underneath
rather nearer the tail than it went in.   But it must be
quite exact the other way.   Remember, it may lean forward
but not sideways.   The best way to be sure of this is to
hold the butterfly quite straight between your thumb and
fore-finger, and then the pin ought to go down exactly,
without the point pricking either of your fingers.   You
may think I am making a great fuss about all this.   But
I am so sure that the only excuse for collecting butterflies
is that they really do look beautiful when well done,
that if you were my boy I would not let you touch them
unless I saw that you took pains with them.   So there !
Now that you have got the pin in straight, the next thing
is to put it straight into the board, *so that the base of the
wings on each side just rests lightly upon the cork.*   You push
the pin generally about a third of the way through, but
this is a matter of taste.   Most boys don't put it through
far enough.   Before we go on, I must describe a little
useful implement for you to make.   Take a wine-cork,
and cut out a square about a small quarter of an inch
every way.   Now get a pretty long fine needle and push

the point into the cork some distance, so that it just goes along one side (in the middle of the side) without coming out. If you have done this as I mean it, you can turn the cork exactly other way up, and then the eye of the needle, and nearly the whole needle, will be lying along the setting board, coming out of the middle of the cork. Hold it like this, and push a strong pin through, straight down, and far enough through the cork to hold

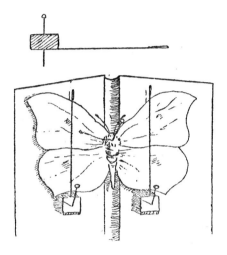

it tight on to the setting board. That's your instrument, and you'll want at least two. Take hold of this by the pin, and with the needle part of it, close to the body of the butterfly, press down the wings, till they touch the setting board, and pin the instrument into the board, tight enough to hold the wings and no more. Do the same with another needle and cork to the wings on the other side. Now with a different fine needle, putting the point into the wing as little as possible, lift or push first

E

the fore-wing, and then the hind-wing, as far up the
board as you think they will look nice and natural.   They
will slip under the needle which is holding them down,
without rubbing off any scales.   Then, when you have
got both sides equal, cut a thin strip of smooth paper :
lay it across the middle of the wings, and pin it tight
across with a pin at both ends, and another a trifle broader
to cover the margin of both upper and under wing and
prevent them from curling.   Don't use your thin expensive pins for these strips of paper, but buy some

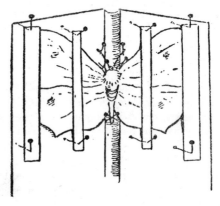

ribbon pins at any draper's shop.   You've nearly done
now—just a pin behind each of the antennæ, to keep them
in their place ; lift the pair of fore-legs on to the edge of
the groove, if you can, with the point of a needle ; and
pin a couple of pins crosswise over the body to prevent
it shifting, near the tail.   You ought to write a date in
pencil somewhere, and not take the specimen off for at
least a fortnight : three weeks is better ; and then you'll
have a specimen good enough to make the only possible
excuse for killing it.   And don't kill any more of that

sort, unless the female is different ; and then only one
more : unless you want one to set, so as to show the
under-side, wrong way up. Three of a sort is the outside
allowance, for only one boy in every ten who begins to
collect, goes on with it as a serious hobby for the leisure
hours of his life. But don't think, when you have done
with a species, as far as your collection goes, that you
need pay no more attention to it. Very far from it.
I hold the actual making of a collection to be the very
smallest part of entomology, and so do the bulk of
collectors who deserve the name. For, apart from the
breeding of insects from the caterpillar, or better still
from the egg, which is so big and interesting a subject
that I am keeping it for a separate chapter, I hold that the
main functions of a naturalist are, not to kill and collect,
though a certain amount of this is necessary, but to watch
the insects and learn their ways : to learn to love their
beauty and the beauty of their surroundings. To become
so familiar with them in fact, that, when the daily papers
talk of the brimstone butterflies hatching early this year,
because they have been seen on a warm day in February,
you will be able to smile, because you know that they
hatched last year, and have been sleeping the cold winter
away in some shelter, and just waiting for this very day,
whenever it may happen to turn up, in order to stretch
their cramped wings a little in the warm sunshine. In
fact I shouldn't wonder if your knowledge might get so
big that you knew even more than this, and could correct
the estimable novelist who talks of " the newly emerged
orange tip and peacock, sunning themselves on the same
Michaelmas daisy " ; displaying thereby a very pretty eye
for colour, but greater ignorance than I hope you will
ever manage to accumulate. I would dearly like to have
you here, two at a time say (I like two boys, but when I
get three or four I turn suddenly into a schoolmaster, and

find my net-stick beginning to tickle my hand), and then
I would take you one day down to the river-side, where
the little clean Bedford blues dance about among the
long grass, and do gymnastics on the swaying stems.
Dainty little acrobats, how I love to watch them! And
aren't they pugnacious too, always fighting and chipping
bits out of each other's wings. The only butterfly that
fights more, to my mind, is the small copper, but he does
not fight so much with his own species—in fact he has
never so many pals to fight with as the Bedford blue—
but with bigger butterflies. He loves most to tease that
sedate old invalid, the wall brown, the dear meditative
old gentleman who flits along the banks a little way, and
then gets tired, and sits down on a warm bit of bare
earth. He does look so bored when that irritating sparklet
of copper and black goes for him. I once saw the little
beggar go for a bee-hawk moth, that had the cheek to
come for a drink to the next pub, a head of bugloss, to
the one which he had chosen for his morning liquor.
The poor moth thought it was a flycatcher at least, and
bolted, leaving the whole bar of both pubs open to the
cheeky little copper. That river-side from which we have
strayed is a lovely place, for when you are tired of watching
the blues, you can tap the tall reeds and out will fly a
vision of brilliant scarlet, a graceful hovering moth that
seems rather pleased to be disturbed, and dips with half-
closed wings down to the water, which he almost seems
to touch, before he rises again, and flickers off into the
reeds on the other side. This is a moth that some of
you will never see, the real scarlet tiger, a cousin of the
clumsy but almost equally showy garden tiger, who lives
in your strawberry beds, and comes out from your woolly-
bear caterpillars. A little farther on, where the yellow-
bedstraw grows, your eye may catch a brilliant spot of
crimson sitting on a stalk. This is the small elephant

hawk moth, with such pretty white stockings on as *you* never wore. Why he should make himself so conspicuous I don't know, unless it is that he is not good for birds to eat. Most of these very showy insects taste nasty, and they are made smart so that birds may remember the look of them, and not be always killing them, and then having to spit them out, dead or cripples and wasted lives. Nature, who seems so very wasteful of life, has got a lot of careful dodges like this, really. That's probably why butterflies have tails to their hind-wings, because when the wings are shut over their backs, then the tails look like the end of their body, which is where a bird tries to grab a butterfly, and so the bird takes the tails in his mouth, and the butterfly gets one more life at any rate. Whether one can argue the good flavour of a butterfly from the length of his tails I don't know.

Most birds, except the real professionals, the swallows and fly-catchers, are extraordinarily clumsy at catching an insect. I had brought half-a-dozen white admirals home in pill-boxes one day, and finding that I did not want them, I opened my window and let one out. He was instantly attacked by six or eight sparrows. It was like putting a worm into an aquarium of minnows. Only they couldn't catch hold of him, and I thought he was going to get off safe, when swish! came fly-catcher, straight as an arrow right through the middle of the sparrows, and bore off my poor admiral, pierced to the very heart, to the nearest croquet hoop. I let the rest go somewhere else. If the butterfly had been a small one, and the bird a swallow, you'd just have seen four bits of wings come fluttering to the ground, all that the swallow had left after that one deadly snap. They are amazingly quick and clean in their butchery.

If we now leave the river, and climb up on to the down, we shall find other blues at various times of the summer, prettiest of all, the chalk-hill blue, with his almost silvery shining wings. Funny how in most of nature it is the gentlemen who wear fancy waistcoats, while the ladies dress very quietly, whereas among men—well, we do run to neckties at any rate. And this is specially to be seen among the blues, where the females are all attired in sober brown, with just a little splash of blue near the body, to show whom they belong to. How I used to tease my sisters about this, and about those female moths who have no wings at all, but who sit at home and are good, while their husbands lark about! Nature is very instructive.

Besides the blues and a few skippers—dingy little fellows with a jerky flight—you will often find in August and September the lovely golden clouded yellow. Some years, when there has been a big spring migration from warmer parts, you will find them in swarms, but there are nearly always a few to gladden the heart of man. And can't they fly! If you miss your shot, you may take a good breath and tighten up your waistbelt, for you'll have a fair field and no favour along those open downs, and it will be very good for you too in that breezy air. You will probably overtake him in a hundred yards in the open. The only better sprinters that I know are a well-trained old male oak eggar moth or emperor. The former I could nearly always overtake in the end, but the latter were always among long heather, and the chase generally ended ignominiously for me, in a full-length sprawl, which knocked all the wind out of me that was left after the run. Of course you can get them both easily by breeding a female from a caterpillar, and putting her in a box of perforated cardboard. They come in swarms and crawl all over you, and a very funny feeling it is to be mobbed and tickled by a lot of moths. But it is rather a shame to catch and kill them, when they have become so tame, and I always thought it fairer to catch the one or two that I wanted after a good run.

The fox moth is another of the same kind and just as hard to catch. All three of them fly a good deal slower about four o'clock in the afternoon. You certainly ought to try bringing them to a female: it is a most extraordinary sight. The wonder is how they know that she is there, but they do, and come in swarms from every quarter of the compass.

Of the other butterflies, you will get some in gardens, but not many. The red admirals, and the peacocks, and tortoise-shells, are generally to be found, either feasting on the fallen apples and plums, or sitting with wide open wings on the asters and other late-summer flowers. In fact, one sees them so regularly there, that I regard them as much part and parcel of an old-fashioned garden, with yew hedges and borders, as I do the other sort of peacocks as the fitting belongings of more stately mansions with stone balustrades and terraces. Hither also come now and then the painted ladies, but they prefer the lanes and waste places, where there are plenty of thistles, and here perhaps once in a lifetime you may see the lordly Camberwell beauty. I saw one once and didn't catch him. It wasn't that I wouldn't, I'm afraid, but I couldn't: I had no net handy, and went for him with my cap, and he flew away in a dignified manner, with me after him, not at all dignified but trembling with excitement, so that honestly I could hardly control my quivering muscles. Down a lane we went, and over a field. I was too anxious, to have another go at him on the wing, hoping that he would settle; I gloated over his gorgeous chocolate and yellow: and then he quietly floated into a great hazel copse, and I saw him no more. I believe I sat down and cried, but I'm not sure: I know I walked the whole way round the edge, hoping that he had strayed out: but he had vanished beyond hope and beyond recall. Curiously enough it happened that this specimen showed itself in the spring, and must have been a hibernated one. One generally hears of them in the autumn. Whether they are any longer native English butterflies, or only get blown over now and then from the Continent, like the bulk of the clouded yellows and painted ladies, is very doubtful. The latter two of course do breed in England, as they are blown over in May, and then lay their eggs, and have an autumn brood. I have bred them both by catching a female in May, and getting her to lay eggs on a sod of clover in one case and a thistle in the other. Anyway I hope you may have the pleasure some day of seeing a live Camberwell beauty. I shall never forget mine, and am almost glad now that I did not catch it.

That is one of my memorable butterfly experiences. Another, and I believe it happened later on in the same year, was that in Nottinghamshire I found, on a fennel plant in the garden, a solitary caterpillar of the swallow-tail butterfly, and I can't make out to this day how it got there. There was no collector within miles, and besides caterpillars don't escape and get into other people's gardens, like live butterflies sometimes do. I have the butterfly in my collection now that came from it ultimately, and it is quite different looking to the specimens which one can still get pretty commonly in the fens of Cambridgeshire. It was a most extraordinary piece of luck. And my one other experience was to find a purple emperor chrysalis by lamplight, while I was hunting moths in the middle of the night in a wood, so high up in a sallow tree, that I had to climb, and then pull a bough down. I happened to turn the light up into the tree to watch a little moth, and it caught my eye. I had just been breeding two or three from caterpillars, and had often gloated over the funny-looking chrysalises, so I suppose the shape and colour were very familiar, and my eye rested on it almost by instinct. I have never before or after seen the insect within ten miles of Winchester. If I'd only got that Camberwell beauty, I should have got, practically by accident, the three most striking, if not perhaps the three actually rarest, of the British butterflies. If you ask me what are the rarest, I really hardly know. I suppose most people would say the Camberwell beauty, the Queen of Spain fritillary and the mazarine blue, but it is so very doubtful whether they can really be called British now, that they have rather lost their interest, exciting though it may be to see a casual visitor of these species on the wing. Personally I would much rather know, as I do, where to go and watch the Glanville fritillaries, disporting themselves by the very edge of the sea-waves, where to find their caterpillars with their pretty pink heads and legs, and little prickly black bodies, feeding on the narrow-leaved plantain, and how to peep under the edges of the big stones that are littered about everywhere, and see their little chrysalises dangling by the tail, ready to come out in a day or two. What with the blue sea and the yellow poppies and the general tangle of other flowers and my pretty little brown butterflies, which can hardly now be found anywhere else in the British Isles, I know very few spots where I'd sooner be alone without you, my young friends. For I hardly trust you yet with my best playthings. But I'll tell you what I'll do. If you'll tell me exactly where I can go and watch the large blues, and all about their caterpillars and chrysalises—or even without these last two, for I'll find them out for myself—I'll tell you where my pretty brown fairies live. Blue eyes for brown eyes is a fair exchange, as many a man has found, myself included.

Well, we've been through my garden, and on to my downs, and along the banks of my trout stream, and into

my lanes I need hardly take you, beautiful though they are
with their hedges full of honeysuckle and clematis, and
their banks covered with wild thyme ; not for the butterflies at any rate, though we will take a ramble there, when
we get on to the moths, for you will not get any that you
don't pretty well know already.   Of course there are the
Bedford blues in the hollows, where the grass grows long
enough to make a wind-swing, but we've seen them by
the river, and there are the orange tips in May, when the
cuckoo plant is in flower, looking hardly English somehow in their brilliant contrast of orange and white.   My
young friends are always bringing me the plainer lady
with no orange on her wings, as befits her more modest
and retiring sex, and declaring that they have caught a
Bath white, another rare visitor that I ought to have
mentioned with the other rather uninteresting rarities.
These too you can breed easily by putting the female
under a bell-glass, with some cuckoo plant in a vase to
lay her eggs on.   The caterpillars will eat the rocket that
grows in old-fashioned gardens.   And it is well worth
doing, if only to see the extraordinary shape of the
chrysalis.   Besides these you will find in the lanes, at
various times, the meadow browns, and their various
rather dull cousins, the other common blues, including
the silver-studded blue, a few skippers, and the green
hairstreak, whose caterpillar, shaped rather like a woodlouse, feeds as often as not upon gorse prickles, of all
funny things to choose for dinner, when there are so
many hundreds of things that look much more edible.
I suppose they mistake it for a sort of giant asparagus.
Fancy an asparagus head that you could climb up and
gnaw the top off, wouldn't it be just ripping !   All these
hairstreaks have little tails to their hind-wings, and if you
watch them while they sit still, they rub their hind-wings
perpetually against one another, to make the tails look

like a waggling little body, for the prying tomtit to seize. There is no doubt that the green hairstreaks must taste nice, for I have caught them over and over again with a neat snip in both hind-wings, where their tails ought to be ; and besides this, look at the colour of the under side, bright green : the butterfly is nearly invisible, when sitting on a leaf, as they often do, and not much more visible when he flies. And you may be sure that the harder any insect is to see, the more the birds like it. It is another of Nature's dodges for saving life, and not quite easy to explain shortly. But just imagine to yourself an insect, nearly equally spotted with black and white. Now if the country and palings were all black, it is probable that those specimens that escaped the birds would be the ones that were a little more spotted with black, and so harder to see than the others. The children of these would be rather darker than the last generation on the whole, and again the darkest would survive, and so the insect would gradually turn black. There is such an insect, the pepper and salt moth ; in fact there are several ; and there is such a black country in the coal districts of England, and in these districts the moths which are speckled black and white in the clean parts of England are now black, and it won't wash off : it is their proper colour. And I want you to get this idea well into the back of your heads, for I shall have to talk about it a good deal when I come to talk about caterpillars. It is one of the many very interesting things which you find out by learning to read the book of Nature carefully.

I've been keeping to the last my nicest domain, and that is my wood and my forest. They are both there, though the king probably calls my forest his. It is where William Rufus ran against an arrow, because he had red hair. And I daresay someone else owns my wood, as far as the pheasants are concerned. But I have bought the butterflies in it from the keeper, at the price of various half-crowns, and promises not to make a row. The same sort of butterflies live in both, even to the purple emperor, for the wood is where I found my one chrysalis. But the scenery is so different that I must really take you just to have a peep at both. We'll go to the wood first: it is a very ordinary little wood, as far as any wood is ordinary. But I know it so well, both in light and darkness, that it seems different in a way. I know just where to go to watch the merry little Duke of Burgundy fritillary; there is a clearing where the hazels were cut down about two years ago, and now they are in neat clumps about a yard high, with plenty of primroses growing all about; here frolics my sportive little duke, round and round the hazel clumps, now sitting for a moment on the leaves, and then off again to play with a duchess. The duke has only four legs and the duchess six, in case you want her to lay eggs, which she will do readily, if you plant a primrose root and put a bell-glass over it. Let her go again, when you can find the little white specks of eggs on the under side of the primrose leaves, and then in about a month you will find that your primrose is looking gnawed about and dilapidated. You won't find any caterpillars by day, because they are down where the leaves join the root, but at night they come up for their dinner, and will probably finish the primrose, and want another, which I should stick in close to the old one, as you will never find all the babies; but in a day or two you can pull out the old root pretty safely, as they will all have gone to the new one. And then at last you will see them crawl up the glass a little way, little brown woodlice, and spin a little silk on the glass, and tie their tails, and run a strand of silk over their fat little bodies, and there they are safe till next May. Only mind you put the glass where no real woodlice can get at it, or your babies will be devoured, for a woodlouse respects neither dukes nor duchesses.

In the same clearing you'll find, much about the same time, only a trifle later, the uncanny-looking bee-hawk moth, hovering over the flowers of the bugloss. His wife is worth keeping for eggs too, with a few sprays of honeysuckle. You'll have to catch her as she hovers, with a downward stroke of the net, as she is pretty active for a stout old lady, and if you once let her get a start, you may say good-bye as politely as your sorrow at parting from her will allow you. Then there are the two small pearl-bordered fritillaries, one about a fortnight after the other, and easily distinguishable by their under sides, and as graceful and pretty butterflies as you will see anywhere, as they float rather than fly from flower to flower. And a sprinkling of green hairstreaks and grizzled skippers will make up the scene into as fair a one as eye could wish to rest upon. Later on in July there are the purple hairstreaks in swarms round the oaks and ashes, almost impossible to catch early in the day, as they are out of reach, but generally coming lower down in the evening. Curiously enough in the case of this species, it is the female who has the smart dash of gleaming purple on the upper wing, while the male is a plain, dull purplish black all over. I wonder why Nature has made this exception to her general rule. I don't believe she ever does anything without a reason, but I am fairly beaten here to discover it.

I have shown you the best of my wood, so now let us go down to my lordly forest. Here everything is on a bigger scale, bigger trees, bigger clearings, great broad rides, and open glades full of stunted holly, and in these latter you shall get the holly blues in April, dancing along from holly to holly. Sit still on a cushion of dead leaves, and watch them come and go, while the wood argus flickers past, a dainty study in sepia and yellow-ochre. You can catch a female of the latter, and put her over a sod of grass, and she will lay her eggs, and give you a fine brood of hungry eaters of grass, who will turn to chrysalises in due season, and hatch out again in the summer, for this is one of the few butterflies which manage to have two broods in the year, a fast style of living which several of the moths adopt.   You may get a few of the holly blues also in my wood, but I preserve them there very carefully, as they are not common.   And I generally have a few even in my Winchester garden : very sacred ones these : thank goodness, most of my young friends don't know they *are* holly blues, though they ought to, as the common blue won't be out for three weeks or a month yet.   But the best time for my forest is June and July.   These rides, where the trees make almost a green arch overhead, with their edges of brambles, are literally alive with white admirals and the big fritillaries.   Sit on the bank opposite that bramble bush in full flower, and watch them come one after the other, and even in twos and threes, the white admirals floating along with hardly a motion of their wings, a very queen among butterflies.   If all ladies moved as gracefully, what a pretty world we should be.   And the great brown fritillaries, full of bustle and energy ; all fighting for the best bramble flower, and literally pushing one another about in their hurry.   And look there at that other strange butterfly, like one of the fritillaries, but glossy bluish black all over, with the black spots showing through ; that's a variety of the female, which you won't find in many places.   Some people say that it is the old original female, and that the present one has gradually developed out of her, so as to be more like her husband. Anyway, if you keep her to lay eggs on a violet root, and manage to get the babies to live through the winter, which is one of the hardest things to do in keeping caterpillars, you will find that a good deal more than half are like their mother, when the butterfly comes out, of the females that is, while the males are all the ordinary ones, and also

the rest of the females. I nearly went wild over the first
of these varieties which I saw. I had never heard of her
before, and thought I had got a most wonderfully beautiful
new butterfly, whose picture was in none of the books,
and whom I could call by my own name, King Hewett.
But my hopes of immortality were shortly afterwards
dashed to the ground by an old gentleman whom I met,
though I was rather soothed in my disappointment by
his obvious desire to have her himself. He was a nice
and kindly old gentleman, such as I should like to be some
day, when I grow up, and told me a great deal that I
did not know about butterflies, and I should like to have
said to him, " Won't you take her ? " but I really couldn't
manage it. I might have done so as I have seen plenty
since, and have reared the caterpillars, and I wish now
that I had, as perhaps he was only down for the day and
never got one after all.

These great glades, full of monstrous oaks and beeches,
are the proper home of the purple emperor. Strangely
enough I have never seen the monarch in his own domain,
soaring round the tree-tops like a great bird, with the
purple gleaming on his wings. But I have bred him,
for the empress lays her eggs on the stinted sallows that
grow here and there in these glades, and on the outskirts,
and one can get the caterpillar by knocking the branches
over an umbrella hold wrong way up, so that he falls
into it, a queer green slug with two horns, not beautiful
to look at ; but one knows what is to come from him,
and values him accordingly, and probably all the more
because you may beat for a great many days without
getting one, and a day's beating, even under a May sun,
is no joke.

Well, my young friends, you know now pretty well as
much as I have to tell you about butterflies, and you will
think, some of you, that my lines have again fallen in
pleasant places. And truly they have, for there is many

a keen naturalist among the factory hands in the North Country who has never had a chance of seeing alive and on the wing much more than half of the beautiful creatures that are around me all the summer.   All that I can plead is, that I believe I am grateful and that I have done my best to appreciate all the beauty that has been showered around me.   I love my whispering river-side ; I love my great breezy downs, where the shadows of the big white clouds race after one another in a good three-mile race : I love my tangled hedgerows with their clematis and honeysuckle and spindlewood : and most of all do I love my grand old forest, where the deer still shed their antlers and the adders slip through the heather, and the otters and badgers steal about at night, and subylla, my queen of butterflies, makes the sun-splashed glades places to lie in and dream.   And if by any talk of all these joys I can wake a kindred spirit in your hearts, or strengthen the spirit that is there already, so that you will walk among such scenes as nature gives you with eyes wide open to see and ears alert to hear and hearts all warm to appreciate and be thankful for those sights and sounds which are a closed book to so many men, I shall feel that I have done something to serve as part payment for all that has been given unto me.

CHAPTER IV

AND MOTHS

THIS has got to be another rather difficult chapter at first, but you're not to skip it, because it is about things that I particularly want you to understand a little, and so you mustn't mind if your brain feels all bulgy for a bit; it will bring out those nice bumps on your forehead, which make the man who has got them look so much smarter than the man who hasn't.

About moths then. The first difficulty is that there are such heaps of them, and the next is that a lot of them are so awfully alike, and the third is their names. Now to take the last first, of course the butterflies are all so well known to us, that it is really quite polite to call them by their Christian names, but the moths are most of them such strangers, that it is generally held more civil to use their unchristian names—names in heathen Latin. Now of course Latin is a bore always, but I cannot help thinking it easier to call a moth a nice simple name like

F

" nemophila," shall we say, than to talk of a " brown-line bright-eye " : and I really don't think you'll find it very difficult to make sure of each one as you get it.   Selene and illustraria don't seem to me very much harder to remember than a great long English name, and I do really advise you to learn the Latin name of every moth you catch. The second of the two names given in the books is the one to learn.   As far as I can in this chapter, however, I will try to stick to the English names, provided I know the moth well enough to take such a liberty.   I have no objection to an oak eggar or drinker, though quercus and potatoria are nearly as easy, but I can't stand a " rustic shoulder-knot," and still less a " merveille du jour," and if I have to mention any of this sort of moths specially, you'll have to take the Latin name with a good grace.

The fact that moths are so difficult to distinguish need not damp your enthusiasm : after all, names are a very small matter : convicts only have a number, I believe : the great thing is to train your eye to see differences of shape and marking ; for your eye can be trained.   Lots of moths that looked very nearly alike when I began, look as different as possible now.   So keep on looking for differences, and keep one or two nice specimens of each sort : and then you can get someone to tell you the names by degrees.

Moths vary much more than butterflies, as you must know, if you have kept drinker moth caterpillars.   There is a light male and a dark male, and a light female and a dark female : and you may fairly keep one of each variety without being extravagant.   Only be always trying to find a reason for differences, if you can, like I showed you in the last chapter about the " pepper and salt " moth, or betularia you might learn to call it for short. Or take another instance in one of the pretty thorn moths

—illunaria. This moth has two broods, one in March and April: these have caterpillars; and there is another brood in July and August, whose caterpillars turn to chrysalises in the autumn, and hatch out in the next March. Now you ought to notice two things about this moth; first, that the spring brood is much larger than the summer brood; and, secondly, that in the spring brood the male is much larger than the female, while in the summer brood the female is distinctly the larger. (In most moths the males have antennæ like ferns or feathers, and the females plain ones.) Now why is this so?—for nature has generally a reason. I suppose the young leaves in May have not so much nourishment in them for the caterpillars as the older leaves in August; this will account for the spring brood being consistently larger: but I can't see for the life of me why the sexes should change size. Can you? Never mind if you can't; it is better to try to notice these kinds of things, and keep a notebook of them for wiser heads to have a try at them, than just to be a mere collector in an un-intelligent sort of way. And besides it makes the bulges grow on your forehead. I do like a boy with a bulgy forehead, not only because he is good at books, but because he does not try to play every ball at cricket in just the same way, but learns that they have to be treated differently, if you want to make a hundred runs: and he is often a cunning bowler too, who tries to find out what kind of balls the other man can't play, and where to put his fields.

Lots of fellows say, " I can't bother about moths: there are such heaps of them." But surely that's very idle and faint-hearted. I grant it is a big thing to go for, but if you are worth anything, you'll not be frightened of a thing because it is big. Most of the things worth doing are big. Only remember, " What's worth doing at all, is worth doing well." I'd rather you didn't do it at all, than go at it in a half-hearted sort of way.

But those of you who are worth talking to, listen to me now and I'll expound. You must get some idea of the principles of division into classes. Of course the rudimentary desire for such knowledge is common. You know the old lady who took a tortoise with her on her travels, and consulted the porter as to what she had to pay, and how he answered, " Dogs is dogs, and cats is dogs, but this is a hinsect and doesn't pay nothing " ; well he had a rudimentary desire to divide things up for the sake of convenience, but I'd like you to get a bit further on than he did. We can begin with butterflies and moths, though that is not nearly the beginning, for bees and spiders and beetles and lots of other things would have to come into the list. A butterfly differs mainly from a moth in having clubbed antennæ, but if you examine closely you will find that the skippers and the burnets aren't so far apart in that way. Still that is the main difference. Some of the old books divided by colours, with the extraordinary result that they put the red admiral in the same class with the tiger moths. The butterflies again are divided up into families. You can see yourself, both from the butterflies themselves, and from their caterpillars and chrysalises, that the red admiral and the tortoise-shells are cousins, and that the wall browns and wood arguses are a different pair of cousins. And when you come to the moths, some knowledge of divisions is quite necessary, if you are to get along. You must at any rate take the privet hawk moth, and the oak eggar, and the yellow underwing, and the brimstone moth, as types of four very different lots, generally known as the Sphinxes, the Bombyces, the Noctuæ, and the Geometers. You will try to get as clear an idea as possible of the main differences between these four, and then you will gradually find that, especially in the two latter classes, you will have to do a lot more dividing, and you mustn't go by the insect alone, but also by the caterpillars and chrysalises and even the eggs, if you want to keep straight. You ought really to have a good microscope, and then the work becomes extraordinarily interesting, and there is a great deal to be done still in this field of labour, if any of you fancy making a name for yourselves in this line. But if you can't go all the way, you must at any rate try to keep your moths in classes. You'll find that the Sphinx caterpillars have tails, that the Bombyces are different sorts of " woolly-bears," that the Noctuæ are naked and fat, and that the Geometers are " stick cater-pillars," who walk by making a great loop in the middle of themselves, because they have only legs in front and behind, and that they let themselves down by a thread out of their mouths. If once you know the caterpillars, you are pretty safe not to make bad mistakes, like putting spinula (the goose egg in English, I believe) among the Pugs, which I have known quite old gentlemen do. But there is more excuse for an old gentleman than for you, because he mayn't be active enough to get the caterpillars, like you are ; and it mayn't suit his rheumatism to be out half the night, as you will have to be now and then for a treat. Curiously enough, that same little spinula who flits about all the hedges at dusk, and whose queer little caterpillar can be beaten into a ' brolly ' almost anywhere, is a very near cousin to the big puss moth, whose caterpillars most of you know and love so dearly. You ought certainly to keep a book of your own making, where you put down all that you can learn about each moth and caterpillar, and particularly try to remember each one as you get it, for they are all different. It sounds a lot, but if you take it just as it comes, a bit at a time, it isn't so very hard.

Now I think you've had pretty nearly enough lecture, but you really ought to try to digest it before you do anything more. Let us go out a-collecting, and I'll take you to some of my pet places. As to collecting moths, there are three principal ways, apart from breeding them from eggs and caterpillars : the first is by good eyesight in the daytime, searching palings and tree trunks and grassy banks ; the second, by giving them a light to fly to—you know how they fly into a room in the evening, and buzz round the lamp and all along the ceiling ; and the third, by putting treacle on the trees. Perhaps one might make a fourth, by beating the bushes and low branches of the trees in the day-time, and it is not a bad way either to get Geometers. One of the great beauties of collecting moths is, that you can get them both by day and by night, and almost all the year round. Of course night is better than day, and summer than winter, but still one can almost always be doing something. The only difficulty is to know when to go to sleep : and it really is rather a serious one, for if you once take to going out for half the night, nothing will stop you, and it becomes a sort of craving that must be satisfied. As dusk approaches, you begin to feel something pulling and tugging at you, and you fancy you hear voices calling you from the darkening woods : little tiny trumpets from ever so far away, they sound like, but you have to go. No matter how much you may have made up your mind not to go, you will find yourself about half-an-hour before sunset, picking up your treacle-pot and knapsack of pill-boxes and stealing away. I say stealing away advisedly, for you should do nothing in a hurry in the evening, if you want really to enjoy yourself. Personally I have a two-mile walk to my sugaring ground, my beloved wood, mostly uphill, but such lovely uphill, through bits of tangled lane, and then out on to a patch

of down, and then in again, while the view spreads farther
and farther back, to the very stalls of the setting sun,
rows of wood interspersed with broad bosoms of down-
land, rising and falling away and away, dimmer and more
mystic as the sunlight fades and vanishes, and sometimes
a little breeze comes creeping along the valley from
Southampton Water, almost smelling of the sea-weed.

Who could hurry on such an evening ?   I know that
the sugar ought to be on the trees half-an-hour after
sunset, but it doesn't much matter ; there is quite enough
of last night's sugar to bring the early moths ; even if
it did matter, why hurry ?   Life is long and wide, as all
this mystic view, and to-morrow will do as well.   Go
slowly and drink in life and peace, and watch the red
orb go down behind the hill, with one tree almost showing
its distant branches against the glowing disc.   Creep
along quietly, and pick up a Geometer here and there
along the lanes.   Net anything that you are not quite
sure of, and don't stop to look.   Pop him into a box
to make excitement for to-morrow's inspection.   If he
is not wanted he can be liberated.   And so we creep on,
and get to the borders of our wood, not so very late
after all, and oh ! so much at peace with all the world.
Cool and still and full of a sort of dreamy anticipation
we feel, as we slowly climb the hurdle that separates us
from the real fairyland.   There are about a couple of
hundred yards to go, between walls of hazel higher than
our head, and everything is as still as the grave, except
for the mystic purring of two goatsuckers, which only
serves to intensify the utter solitude and aloofness of
everything.   We greet a rabbit or two that scurry along
the path, nearly invisible but for the flicker of a white
tail, with almost a feeling of gratitude for companionship.
And yet it is very beautiful, after a day's worry, to soak
oneself in this utter loneliness, like sinking down into

deep waters, with the moonlight and starshine coming
through. And now the light is dying, as we emerge
from our path, into an almost more solitary clearing,
with just big trees standing at intervals, and little bunches
of hazel looking like animals feeding among them, and
beyond and away the mysterious recesses of the thicker
wood. Here we have a round of trees to re-sugar, where
we have come for many nights, as the black patches on
their trunks testify. Drop a little essence of pine-apple
or jargonelle into your treacle, to make it more attractive,
and light your lamp, for we shall find a few early feeders
already on the old patches. Get all round with your
fresh treacle as quick as you can, picking off into boxes
anything that looks attractive, and then—I was going to
say "light your pipe," but that won't do—well, watch
me light mine, and sit on a felled tree trunk, and wait

for half-an-hour. We need not really wait for more than
ten minutes, as the moths know where to come. A
round of sugar gets better and better every night. But
I do love that wait. Now and again you catch a glimpse
of the goat-suckers hawking about, and wonder if they
are getting all your best moths, and all the while the
darkness gathers in, and seems to settle down upon you
like a thick fog, so that you breathe more and more quietly,
for fear of breaking some magic spell, and the little mice
rustle round you in the grass, and the rabbits creep about
—and one night I even watched a badger in the distance,
and had hard work not to believe him to be a bear, as
he grunted and poked about—and then at last the owls
begin to call. What they remind me of I don't know :
but it is something to do with lost souls, not very unhappy,
but just wanting something that they can't quite find,
and would be quite happy if they only could find it.
Lovely old woolly men ! Someone loves the spring
calling of the curlew, someone loves the bleating of the

snipe, someone loves the plover on the downs or in the fallows, and well do I love them all too, and well do I love the goat-sucker, who runs down like a clock, and makes everything feel creepy, and well do I love the corncrake, when he doesn't keep me awake too long at night; but most of all, I think, do I love my owls. They seem to take me further away than any of the others from everything troublesome, into a land of romance and possibilities. Into the land where the golden key lies at the foot of the rainbow, and where the shadows meet and talk without voices, because they all understand just what the others want without any talking : into the land where nothing grows old, because everything is so old and peaceful, that it has become young again, and can feel the happiness and joy of youth, without its frettings and anxieties to grow older, and can feel the calm and rest of age, without the stiffening of the muscles and the pining for the lost blessings of youth. I am looking hard for the land, and the owls take me nearer to it than any of the other birds, though they all try to show me the way. But when the owls begin to call it is time to be up and doing. And what a wonderful sight it is on a good night, as you carefully turn your light on to a black and shining patch of sugar. Carefully it should be done, especially when the " crimson underwing " are about, for they and one or two others are very shy, notably the lovely batis and derasa, sitting with their wings half-parted, and ready to be off into the darkness ; but most of the others are very sluggish, and will almost fall off into a pill-box. Take an old postcard in your pocket : pop the box over the one you want most, then slip the card under and take the box carefully away ; pop the lid over, and slip the card out and mind you keep your full and empty boxes in different places. You will also have to note carefully which moths sit quiet all night

in a pill-box, and which must be killed at once, for some
will spoil themselves. These latter must be taken off
the tree into a cyanide bottle, and pinned sideways, and
pricked with oxalic acid at once, and put into a box with
damp cork directly you get home. You will have to
learn by experience which are which, in the way of sitting
still.   And also remember that now is the time to
catch and keep alive females to lay eggs. You ought
to get and rear quite sixty caterpillars from every female
that you keep, and, besides the extra beauty of bred
specimens and possible varieties, you have the pleasure
of turning out into liberty a lot of moths, who would
otherwise certainly have been eaten in the caterpillar
or chrysalis stage by the birds, and then you feel that
you have made some amends for the lives you have taken.
I believe that on a reasonable calculation I have saved
nearly as many moths as I have killed. One has to keep
some of the better ones generally to exchange for others
that one has no chance of getting oneself. But I never
cared greatly for these moths got by exchange : I knew
nothing about them. Exchanging caterpillars is more
interesting, when you can do it.

To come back to our trees. The first thing probably
that you will notice is a long black or brown snail or
two, then a fringe of earwigs, and possibly a hornet or
two. Then you will realise that all the moths have little
scarlet eyes. Very pretty these miniature rubies are in
every head, and the long proboscis quivering over the
sugar. A moth is very careful to keep his feet clean,
and sits on the dry bark, reaching out for the sugar like
an elephant. Don't be in a hurry to take any, unless
they are obviously ready to go. Look them over first
for possible rarities. You never know what may come
to sugar. That is one of the joys of it. You will take
two or three specimens of a moth one night that you

have never seen before, and you may see no more of them that year, or the next, or ever again. It has happened to me several times. When you have made a careful selection round the patch, then work down the trickles, where the sugar has run down the trunk; some moths always like these best; and you will find a few that have dropped off on to the ground when the light was turned on to them. I don't think they are drunk, only shamming dead. And you are not the only person who comes to look for them. I have seen a mouse run away from the foot of a tree with a moth in his mouth, and I have also seen an owl pop down out of the dark and apparently and presumably get the mouse. All these creatures are very tame and fearless in the dark, if you only work quietly, and you will see many pretty sights. There were two hedgehogs one year that always came for a moth or two, and even a toad camped at the foot of one tree for many nights to take his share of the spoil. Most of the moths are Noctuæ, but a few Geometers come pretty regularly, notably dolabraria, extersaria, and repandata, and if you are sugaring in the open, the small elephant hawk moth will come for a drink, but he never settles; he takes it, like the humming-bird moths drink of the geranium flowers, and looks very smart in his cerise and yellow livery and white stockings. I don't think I can give you a list of all the moths that you may take at sugar. It would be rather long and very dull. You may imagine almost anything in the way of Noctuæ. And this imagining is part of the delight of it. You ought to go certainly twice round your trees, and then the best is over. I believe they begin to come again, about one or two in the morning, but I always wanted some sleep before that, and I don't advise you to stay. So make everything snug for the home journey, and pick up your net, and get a few Geometers on the way home, as they flutter across the path of light that your lantern makes. The big emerald is the most beautiful of them all, and I generally got him in this way until I learned how to find his caterpillars, and then I didn't bother about him, and he used to come and sit on the very lamp in my hand. I carried one half-way home once in this way. I wonder whether she ever found her husband again, for he was a she : I hope she stayed where I left her, and made a new home. All these insects are rather stay-at-home. You will find the marbled white butterfly in the same field year after year and in no other, and then suddenly there comes a year when for no very apparent reason they are all about the country-side. One of the fritillaries, artemis, generally only lives in two fields five miles away from here, but three years ago she came into the Winchester water-meadows, and even on to our cricket-field ; and now she is back again in her old place and nowhere else.

It's funny work walking home. When you come out of the wood you feel as if you had suddenly stepped into the ordinary world again, and then you gradually go to sleep. I believe I slept half the way home generally. I often found myself first in the hedge on one side and then in the hedge on the other. Luckily there were no ditches. I believe to this day that I began to stumble over a stone directly I got out of the wood once, and kicked that stone all the way into Winchester. And then a cow snorts at you over a gap, and you wish she hadn't. The cock pheasants in the wood were bad enough when you startled them. I used to implore them not to crow till I got out of the wood ; but a cow is far worse. One feels so empty inside when that sort of thing happens. But otherwise it is very jolly, snoozing along downhill, and getting sometimes a sniff of honey-suckle and sometimes a sniff of elder, and sometimes

passing through a stream of extra warm air, and then
through a cool stream : and then you hear the night mail
coming from Southampton, and watch the streak of fiery
smoke come racing along the valley, and so you find
yourself home, and after a drink, and perhaps a piece of
cold plum-pudding or apple tart which some thoughtful
person has put out, and which never spoils your sleep
when you eat it as late at night as that, you sneak off to
bed, looking forward happily to a review of your boxes
in the morning.

I hope that this brief description will give you some
idea of what a night's sugaring can mean. Of course I
could not go every night to the wood ; it meant getting
home so late, and I had nearly always to be up at half-past
six. But I generally went off somewhere. Out on to
the downs, where there was a row of palings, where the
lane gradually opened into the down. One got generally
some Noctuæ here different from the wood-dwellers, but
it was not such pretty work. The best insect here was
one of the yellow-underwings called subsequa, just like
the ordinary small one, only with the same black spot
in the corner of his upper wing that the big one has.
Funny that one spot should make the difference between
a very common insect and quite a rare one ! But it is
all right : I have bred them both right through from
eggs laid by a female with the spot, and by one without
it, and all the children were like their respective parents.
One advantage of going to this place was that one could
have a go at the Geometers in the lane between whiles,
so that there was variety at any rate as well as earlier
bed.

I never worked Light scientifically. The thing is to
have a white sheet stretched between two poles, which
stick into the ground, and a big lamp on a stand, shining
on to the sheet. The whole thing is rather like a magic-

lantern before the picture goes in, and then the moths come and sit on the sheet, and you net them.   I believe it is very effective, and ought to be quite pretty work, but I never could summon up courage to start out with all that paraphernalia, and plant myself in full view of Winchester.   I always had a liking for stealing about quietly on my business, and so, as far as light went, I contented myself with pottering about the street lamps in the suburbs with a net and some pill-boxes, but this was also too public to be really nice.   Someone or other was always passing by, and the policeman looked on distrustfully, and I do so hate the feeling that I am regarded as a harmless sort of lunatic.   That is partly why my wood is so pleasant a place.   You are all by yourself, and have not to bother about anyone else.   If you have a house in the country, however, it is a great thing to put a light in an upstairs window, and have another good one in the room, and sit there with a net and a book.   On warm still nights you will reap a fine harvest.   Even the great hawk moths come in, and lead you a rare chase round the room, which obviously ought to have as little furniture in as possible.

Talking about hawk moths, have you ever caught the convolvulus hawk moth ?   I never had until I was told how he loved the tobacco plant.   And then I planted a bed full, and watched them every evening at dusk, beginning about the last week in August.   Nothing happened for two or three nights, and then I was conscious of a presence in the garden ; I never actually saw anything, but I was quite sure that something was on the move. I had on rather a brilliant cricket coat, and suddenly, against my very sleeve, I was conscious of a big moth hovering with a long proboscis, trying to get honey out of my coat.   Never before or after was I mistaken for a flower, to my knowledge.   I could see his eyes.   There was nothing for it but to keep still, and I eyed him covetously, while he strolled round me, looking for honey. Finally he gave it up, and for half-an-hour dodged me round that bed of tobacco plant. Now and then he came for a little cruise round my head, and once I felt his wings. Finally having kept me in great agony and excitement he went away, and I tried to drown my grief with supper. Next night he came again and brought a pal with him, to make it up, I suppose, for I caught the pal at once ; I'm sure it was my pal's pal, for the other continued to keep a cautious eye on my movements, and always contrived to have the bed between me and him. Next night there were none, but the night after there came two again, and again I caught one pretty easily, and the other kept well away, as though he had done his duty to me for my kindness in planting the tobacco plant by bringing me two specimens for my collection, and meant also to do his duty to himself in keeping well out of reach of my net. I saw him nearly every evening after that for a long time, but I never got him. I confess I went for him rather half-heartedly, for I loved him dearly. Sometimes, when it got nearly dark, I could only tell where he was by the movement of the white flowers, where his great wings fanned them, and it was funny to see this movement wander round the bed, as I edged towards it, like a row of bells set ringing one after the other. I wonder if they breed in England ; I only ever caught one at all looking like a newly emerged specimen, and they often catch them in the lighthouses on the South Coast, which looks as if they flew over from a warmer place. A very old book that I saw treated them as common moths, and said that the caterpillar fed on the bindweed growing in the corn-fields. I believe they mostly fly across on those great narrow wings of theirs. They would come almost as

easily as a swift.   Anyway I hope you'll see one some
day, for they are the finest of all the moths.   I saw one
last August close to Cape Wrath, if you know where
that is, so that they evidently wander very far north.
I went for him with a landing-net, just for the sake of
old acquaintance, but he easily dodged me.   I'm afraid
he couldn't have been my old pal, but he may have been
a grandson : he was very wary and wide awake.

Finding moths by good eyesight, or rather, trained
eyesight, and pretty accurate knowledge of their habits,
always strikes the unskilled person as the most wonderful
performance.   But it isn't really.   Of course, the moths
are generally very like what they sit on, but after a while
they seem to catch the eye : so much so that I have often
been mouching along, half asleep, and have suddenly
remembered that I believed I saw a moth twenty yards
back, and have retraced my steps and found him : and
yet I have shown people the same moth, and they could
not see him till my finger almost touched him.   This
resemblance of moths to what they sit on is one reason
why you ought to do a little exchanging.   Let me
illustrate by an instance.   There is a little Noctua called
perla, whitish with grey markings.   He sits on walls in
the daytime, because his caterpillar—a funny little midget
—feeds on the lichens on the walls, and runs into holes
in the mortar like a rabbit for safety, when he isn't feeding.
He's a terribly difficult one to keep, because the lichen
gets either too dry for him or too wet, if you keep him
in a pot.   But I have got him to live sometimes.   Well,
you see the wall is the gentleman's home altogether,
and so he sits on it.   And as in some parts of England
the wall lichens are very pale, he is very pale there, because
the specimens most like the lichens in colour have escaped
the birds and had children and so on.   In other parts of
England, the lichens are yellow, and the specimens there

are conspicuously yellower than the others, while yet again, where the lichens are greener, you will find perla with an obviously green tinge over him. People used to think that moths changed colour like the chameleon is still said to, at their own sweet will, but they only change by districts ; though, when I come to talk of the caterpillars in the next chapter, I shall have one or two awkward problems to put to you, which make one wonder how far this theory of the natural survival of those most like their surroundings can account for all the changes. Another interesting moth in this way is called cinctaria, a Geometer which sits on the dwarf pine trunks among the heather at Lyndhurst. Its caterpillar feeds on the heather : that's why the moth sits there. And it is one of the very hardest to see, as it spreads out its wings, and presses them flat against the trunk, which it exactly resembles in its reddish-brown colour, with a little dark grey mixed in with the brown. But here and there you find one much lighter, with almost white bars in the wings, which is quite easy to see. This moth has two near cousins, roboraria and consortaria, which live among the birches, and sit on the trunks in the same way, and are both quite pale. Now I have very little doubt that in old days, before the thirsty pines were brought in to drain the place by drinking up the moisture, the little trees spreading out into the heather wilderness were all birches, as the birch is one of the original inhabitants. And in those days cinctaria were pale, but as the pines pushed the birches out, it didn't pay to be pale, and so they got more and more like the pines, till they reached their present state of perfect resemblance, all but a few who are old fashioned, and hark back to their original ancestors, as things will for a long time after the fashions of those ancestors have changed. The green moths, on the other hand, like the emeralds, sit on the leaves, also

G

with their wings flat against the surface. Not, I think,
because they know that it is safer to sit on the same colour
as themselves. But because, from always sitting on the
leaves, they have grown like them in the way I have
mentioned. All these that I have been describing to you
escape notice by squashing themselves close down on to
whatever they sit on. But some of the dull coloured ones
sit with their wings up, to look like a dead leaf blown
against the trunk, or stuck in the grass, and you will
find that most of these do not have the edge of their
wings smooth and regular like most of the moths, but
cut into jagged shapes and queer curves. The best
examples of this method of escaping notice are several
of the hawk moths, particularly the poplar, lime and
eyed hawks, and all the thorn moths. All of these have
shaped edges to their wings, and sit with their wings in
variously raised positions. How the comma butterfly
has got the extraordinary edges to *his* wings, I can't say :
not more than any other butterfly at any rate. The
autumn moths again show a great tendency to run to
yellow, as, for instance, all the Xanthia family, who sit
about presumably among the fallen leaves. I say presumably, partly because they are this colour, and partly because
you don't find them sitting on any of the trunks or palings.
Citrago, I know, sits among the fallen leaves of the limes,
for I have found it there. On the other hand there are
a few moths visible from anywhere which seem to court
observation. Probably these are not nice to eat, and
advertise the fact accordingly, to save their bacon, like
the danger-flag of yellow and black which the wasp hoists.
It is curious how cautiously a spider goes for any brilliantly
coloured insect that comes into his web, holding it at
arm's length, and turning it round hurriedly with the
very tips of his toes. All the more curious because wasps
so very seldom get into their webs, and if they do, are

out again directly.   One wonders how in the world they know.   I suppose that one of their ancestors was once killed accidentally by a wasp, or killed in deadly combat, and the young spiders all have to learn it in their histories of Spiderland, and get punished if they don't know the dangerous colours.

I don't think that I have any very special information of a general kind to give you, on the subject of trunk and paling hunting, beyond the advice to do it by all means, even if you don't find much at first.   You will soon train your eye into ability to see the moths.   Only don't look on the side that the sun catches, for a moth can't bear to sit in the sun, nor again is it much use looking on the windy side, as they don't like having their wings blown about.   If there is sun on one side and wind on the other, it is not a great deal of good looking, except on very rough trees, where they can get into the cracks in the bark.   And also remember that you must not look for grapes off thistles.   That is, that moths as a rule don't go very far from their food-plant.   So you will find demas coryli and fagi sitting principally on beech trunks ; roboraria, as I have said, specially among the birches.   The only exception is pine trees.   I always go for all solitary pine trees, and they very seldom cheat your hopes.   It is the rough bark I suppose.   As to the height on the trees, there is no rule that I know, except ' The worse the day, the lower the moth.'   In very fine still weather, you may often see them out of reach.   I did quite a big climb for fagi once, but she was well worth it, for she laid sixty eggs, and I bred forty moths from them.   As to palings, I always cast an eye on them, but I specially love a row of upright posts, holding barbed wire, on the top of the downs.   There I get the great privet hawk moth, with his dull grey upper wings alone showing, exactly the colour of the old palings, but big enough to be rather visible : serena visible for thirty yards, generally within six inches of the top—she must taste very nasty ; umbratica much less visible about half-way up ; and a great lot of casual Noctuæ right at the bottom, where the grass has grown round the paling, and makes a fine shelter. You just push it aside, and there you see them sitting, twiddling their antennæ to find out what is the matter.

It remains only to say a little about times and seasons, and then you ought to be pretty experienced moth-hunters. I have said that there is something to do almost all the year round, and you will find this to be true. On fine days in January, unless there is a big frost on, you may go to the woods, and knock about where the old beech leaves still cling to the stunted bushes, and you are almost sure to get leucophearia, a pretty sepia and white Geometer, with a nice variety where the sepia is dark and runs into blotches, and the white is in bands. Don't go on a windy day, or they will get blown away before you can catch them. In February pilosaria sits on the trunks, and also hispidaria, both rather large and heavy bodied for Geometers, with wingless females. In March, on sunny days, you can net the gay parthenias among the birches ; it flies lower towards four o'clock ; and in early years the sallow blossoms are out at the end of the month, bringing a rich harvest. Hold an inverted umbrella underneath, and tap the trunk, and you will get a regular shower of tæniocampidæ, and other Noctuæ. In April the sallows are still out, and you may begin to watch the palings. May, I generally devoted to cater-pillar hunting. June to November are the great sugaring months, when light ought also to be worked. Late in November, and early in December, you can take P. populi on the lamps, and keep a female for eggs, which hatch in March and feed on willow or sallow, and all through

December there is the little winter moth brumata, that does such harm to the apple-trees. That is enough to show you that there is always something to do, and I only hope that I have made the subject attractive enough to lead some of you to take up the study : even if you don't take to collecting—and I'm not very anxious that you should—it is an endless source of pleasure, to know a good deal about the lives and ways of all these creatures. There is rather a tendency nowadays among boys to concentrate their interests on cricket and the bigger amusements ; but my great hope is that, as these bigger amusements are becoming so serious in their methods, as to be almost on the same footing as work, there will arise a demand for the lighter relaxations of natural history. As long as a boy was allowed to hit ' blooming hard and blooming high and blooming often ' I had very little hope, but now that this dissipation is forbidden, there does seem to me some chance of getting him to take an hour off now and then for the less exacting amusement of moth-hunting. I always have a high opinion of Solomon, as a man who held sound views about how to enjoy himself, and I expect that he got his reward in that way somehow from taking the trouble to know about the hyssop on the wall.

CHAPTER V

CATERPILLAR REARING

My earliest experiences are mixed up with caterpillars. I can hardly remember the time, when I didn't delight in them. And I doubt whether, even in my days of ripest experience, my caterpillars ever had a better time than had those pets of my infancy. I hope, when you are my age, that you will be able to say the same. I lit upon an old fern case with glass sides. This I filled with soil, to a depth of about three inches, and planted here and there a nice clean little root of grass, and stuck in sprigs of hawthorn and beech and willow, with a large dandelion in the middle, and gave the whole a good watering. Then I sallied forth to hunt the banks and hedgerows, and, after about an hour, returned with a handkerchief containing various caterpillars of the tiger moth, drinker, and oak eggar. Well do I remember finding my first caterpillar of this latter species, and my delight over a new specimen. I am afraid that he did not feel equal pleasure for a time, for, at that period, my fern case only contained grass and dandelion, and, as I found him on a stem of dry grass at the top of the bank, it did not enter into my head, that he could be so foolish as to belong really to the prickly hedge, and to have just come down, either to change his skin or to bask in the sun. I knew, of course, that hedge buds were very good to eat. All boys know that, I fancy ; but I only associated caterpillars with grass and dock and dandelion. So he was brought home in triumph, and put with the rest. That was at about 2 p.m., and at about five my menagerie was always taken for a walk on the glass of the cucumber frame, where fresh dainties were laid out for their delectation. Bunches of grass for the drinkers, and docks and dandelions and nettles for the tigers. Tea and shrimps, so to speak.

My new beast behaved badly : he wouldn't look at his food, and showed no desire to take a stroll. However, as I had had measles only the year before, when I could eat nothing but buttered biscuits, I concluded that he must be sickening for something of the sort, and put him back to bed. In the night, he found time to do what he wanted, and changed his skin, looking very smart in the morning, with his new suit of grey, and black belts at his various waists, and a fine reddish cap on his head. I was so pleased with him, that I gave him a special walk all to himself, and piles of butter and eggs for breakfast, but he would have none of them. He walked miles, poor old man, over that glass frame, getting a bigger appetite every step he took with every leg, and I was charmed with his energy, though distressed at his refusing his " wittles." I put him away again, and ransacked the hedgerows for juicy herbs, not having any book to guide me, and this went on the whole day.

Next morning, he looked so ill and worn out, having probably walked all night, while the others were munching their suppers, that I did one of the wisest things, in my distress, that I ever remember to have done. It pleases me even now to think of it, and I pat myself on the head. I took him to the place where I found him, and told him to help himself, and watched him climb the hedge, to my amazement. Then he got a leaf edgeways between his fore-paws, and didn't he just slice it away, strip after strip, till the leaf was done, the last slice falling away, as he bit it through near the bottom. He looked longingly after it as it fell, and then went for another leaf : but I had other things to do : the day was never long enough in those happy times, and now the night is never long enough. And besides, I had read that starving people, who had been rescued from boats, as I meant to be rescued some day, ought never to be allowed to eat too much at a time. So I took him away, and cut off one or two lovely sprays from the hedge, and put him back with the others : and, after just waiting to see him climb one, and set to work, I left him. He became a great pet, and I found that he liked beech leaves, and fairly loved willow, and, after spinning a grand hard oval cocoon, which I could play with, he came out into one of my old friends the oak eggars, who had given me so many fine races across the lawn and meadow. I let him go, and caught him again in my net, just to teach him what perils lay in his path, and that he must hurry up when he went for a fly, and then let him off for good.

It was one of his successors, a lady this time, who showed me how to bring the gentlemen, as I described to you in the other chapter. I was playing with her on the lawn, and wondering why she didn't fly, when the gentlemen came one after the other. So that, when I read about it afterwards in a book, I was able to think that I knew all about it, without being told, which is always nice.

For a long time, I could not help opening my cocoons, to look at the chrysalises, which is a good thing in itself, because one ought to know what they are like, and also the cocoons are so funnily made, some of them with lids, and some with two distinct layers of stuff. But it was a bad thing in another way, because when the chrysalises began to get soft and crackly, I could not resist trying to help them out. I had seen my mother chip away the shell from an egg, to help the chicken out, and it seemed much the same thing to chip away the shell of a chrysalis, and get out first a live antenna, that waggled, and then a leg that pawed the air, and at last the whole body. And sometimes it was all right, and the moth climbed up a stick, and you could watch his wings gradually grow, all puffed out at first, and then folded straight over his back, like a butterfly, and then, after about half-an-hour, when they were quite dry, down they folded by his side, and he was ready to fly, or some- times, I am afraid, to be killed. But often, until I learnt patience, I helped him too soon, and he died, with his poor little wings, with their tiny distinct pattern, all unfolded. So be advised, and let them alone. Only mind you remember to give them something to crawl up. They can't get up the glass side of a fern-case. They must be able to hang their wings down, to grow them properly. And a word more about the keeping of them. One cannot always have glass fern-cases. What they want most is fresh air, cool air, plenty of fresh food, plenty of room, and I always think that they like to have a watering-can held over them for a minute now and then, just like plants. Now, I always keep them in good large flower-pots, with plenty of drainage, and muslin or unbleached calico tied over the top. Fill the pot

half-full of earth, in case they want to bury themselves,
and, if they do bury, you may dig them up in a fortnight,
but not any sooner, and lay the chrysalises on moss in
a box or flower-pot ; but always damp the moss now
and then, and let them have plenty of air. If you happen
to dig any up before they have turned, don't bury them
again, but lay them on the moss with the chrysalises,
and they will probably turn all right. It is a most wonderful thing to dig up a privet moth caterpillar, after he has
buried, and watch him turn to a chrysalis. You can
hardly see the transformation begin. The old skin splits
at the head, and then gradually works off, leaving a very
soft squashy green thing, with all the marks of the caterpillar's legs on it, and this gradually hardens to the fine
shiny brown thing which perhaps you know. Mind you
tie the cloth over the top of the pot tight enough, or
they will squeeze out under the string ; and look out
for earwigs getting in, for they eat caterpillars for
breakfast and lunch and dinner. And don't try to keep
too many in one pot. Six big ones like the tigers are
enough. I know of one gentleman who keeps them all
in tumblers, one in each. But surely they must be lonely,
and just think of the feeding of them ! If ever you find
one that you don't know, try him with birch and
groundsel : there are very few caterpillars that won't eat
one or other. But don't water those that eat groundsel
or squishy plants, or they'll go bad. These ought to be
kept as dry as possible. I even dry the food, if I have
to get it on a wet day.

There are various ways of getting caterpillars. When
you first begin, the nicest way is just to look out for them
on the banks and hedges. You won't get a great many
sorts, but you don't want a great many just at first. But
when you have learnt how to manage them nicely, then
you can try some of the more elaborate ways. Far the

best—though it is the most difficult, and perhaps I ought not to begin with it—is keeping a moth to lay eggs. If you have the microscope I talked about, mind you look at the eggs. No two are alike, and they are most beautiful things, lots of them like little jellies, looking awfully good to eat : others like shells, all ribbed and crinkled : others like jars full of coloured drinks. A female will generally lay her eggs on the side of a pill-box, but some, who tuck them into crevices in the bark, like a little loose cotton-wool and bits of crumpled paper. Perhaps the best way of all, if the caterpillar feeds on a tree, is to make a little muslin bag, and put her in that, and then slip the end of a branch in, and tie the mouth of the bag tight round the stem of the branch. Then she can either lay her eggs on the leaves, or in the crinkles of the muslin. Mind you untie the bag very carefully, for the eggs are often in the crinkles close to the string. If you keep her for more than one night, give her a drop of treacle, only one, on the outside of the bag. She'll drink through the muslin, and you can watch her proboscis at work. Or if she's in a box, put a very small drop on a bit of cotton-wool.

When the caterpillars feed on groundsel, or such like things, I often put a leaf of that in the box ; and sometimes with butterflies, I put a bell-glass over a little root of the food in the shade. A clouded-yellow goes over a sod of white clover, a wood-argus over a little sod of grass, a Duke of Burgundy over a primrose root, and a silver-washed fritillary over a violet root. You can't very well miss the eggs—little green or white or crimson globules, sometimes laid separately, sometimes in strings. The funniest of all are those of the emerald called vernaria, whose caterpillar feeds on the wild clematis. She lays her eggs in strings, like little green cheeses one on the top of the other. They look exactly like a tendril of the clematis twisted round and round, and I have no doubt she does it on purpose, so that they shall be mistaken for one ; but how does she learn to do it ? You can tell the females of the Noctuæ by their fatter bodies, and of the Geometers by their plain antennæ, the males wearing plumes. I never keep a female, except under very special circumstances, for more than two nights. If she hasn't laid then, she has most likely laid her eggs before you caught her. After a day or two, the eggs change colour. If they don't change, you may be pretty sure that they are bad, and won't hatch. And in about ten days most of them hatch, except a few autumn ones that go through the winter, and hatch in the spring. You can tell when they are going to hatch, by their turning nearly black (most of them), and when they hatch, your troubles begin.

Those that feed on an easy tree are best managed by leaving them in the muslin bag, only mind it is very close muslin, or they will squeeze out through the tiny holes ; and look out for earwigs, for they soon find them out, and gnaw a hole in the muslin. When they have eaten up the twig in the bag, you cut it off, and, if they are big enough to manage, shift the bag on to another : but if they are still very tiny, open the bag wide, and put the whole thing—bag, tiny caterpillars and all—into a bigger bag, and tie that on to a fresh branch, and, in a day or two, they will have all found their way out on to the new leaves, and you can untie the string and pick out the old bag empty. That's all fairly easy. But those that can't be put in bags are a sore trial at first. I get a little bottle at a chemist's, about two inches high, with a neck as wide as the bottle, and put in a little bit of food, groundsel, or whatever it may be. Then, with a paint-brush, I carefully sweep the herd of tiny caterpillars out of the pill-box into the bottle, and tie a bit of very fine muslin over the mouth. Now watch the little beggars, and see how they worry the food. Poor little kiddies! They can hardly stand, but they are evidently born with teeth. Next morning your troubles are well on you. Take a sheet of white paper, and tilt the bit of food out. Lucky for you if plenty of the caterpillars are left sitting on the sides of the bottle! Now pick up the food-plant gingerly with a pair of tiny tweezers, and tap it carefully over the paper. Some of the caterpillars fall off, but a lot, sometimes all, dangle on threads, and these worry the life out of you, before you get them all safely into the bottle, on to the new bit of food. Finally, you sweep the white paper into the bottle with the paint-brush, and then tap the old bit of food again, for a fresh supply, until you get most of them in. Perhaps it is simpler to tilt the whole thing into a rather bigger bottle, with some fresh food in it, but you are bound to come to the trial of a complete house-clearing once or twice, before they are big enough to handle. And you don't know what worry is till you have tried it. You see, there are probably over a hundred of them. Of course, unless they are very rare ones, you can be content with two or three dozen, and turn the rest out on to their food in the wilds at once, but I generally think it rather unkind to send them out into the world until they have grown a bit. After all, they grow very quickly, and soon want larger quarters, first a small jam-pot, then a larger one, and then the final flower-pot. But, especially when they are tiny, keep the nursery in a cool shady place, or else the moisture off the food-plant condenses on the side of the bottle, and they get drowned; and keep them clean, or they will die of various diseases.

That will give you, I hope, some idea, in a very brief form, of the difficulties and delights of breeding from the egg, and of the general method of keeping small caterpillars. I must now try to describe some of the other ways of getting them, or their chrysalis. But they all fall short in one important point, and that is, that a great percentage of what you get in the wilds will be useless, because the ichneumon flies have already laid their eggs in them. It is a great trial to open the pot one morning, and to find your caterpillar a flabby husk, all eaten away by these pests. And breeding from the egg saves you from this trial at any rate.

There are three great ways of getting caterpillars, if not more—Beating, Sweeping, Searching. For the first, you want an old umbrella and a longish tough stick. Regular beating trays are sold, which have their advantages, but an umbrella does very well, though it is rather difficult to hold upside down, and a few caterpillars get damaged by falling on the hard ribs. The process is simple. You hold it under a likely branch, and tap the stem of the branch smartly with your stick, and the caterpillars fall into the umbrella. *Sweeping* requires a net like a butterfly net, only made of coarser and stronger material like butter-cloth, with the stick running right across the mouth and into the far side to strengthen it, and the ring, to which the bag of the net is fastened, is made also of something stronger then the cane of the ordinary net. You can buy them, but they are not very difficult to make. With this net you sweep the low-growing herbage, heather, etc., in the late evening, and it is hard work, but productive of rich results. *Searching* consists in going out with a lantern at night, and investigating the low bushes and banks, and has all the attractions of night-work, besides training the eyes. You can get a good deal too in this way in the daytime, if you know how to set to work. Besides these three, I must mention digging and searching for chrysalises.

Now, as you won't get a very clear idea from a mere

enumeration of methods, I'd better take you out on an imaginary journey or two, in quest of booty. And I think I shall very likely have to cram a year's journeys into a day : I mean that we shall get, on one imaginary journey, caterpillars which are found at different times of the year. I will tell the months, as far as I can, on the way. But you may take it roughly, that May and September to October are the great caterpillar seasons. Take your beating-tray or umbrella then, and we'll start off on a nice still day in May. A windy day is bad, because it is so hard to hold the tray ; and the smaller caterpillars get blown sideways, as they fall, and miss the tray ; and a wet day is hopeless, because you get a shower-bath out of every branch. The sallows—you know the tree rather like a willow that bears the yellow palms at Easter—are just nicely in leaf, and it seems a shame to beat them. Don't pick the cleanest-looking ones, for caterpillars soon make a tree look scrubby. And don't neglect the little tiny ones that grow just on the sides of the rides in the woods. Put your umbrella on the ground, and bend the whole little tree over it, and tap the stem hard and sharply. It may happen, if you are on your lucky day, that you will find a green caterpillar, like a small slug, with two horns on his head, wondering where he has fallen to, and turning his head first to one side and then to the other. Take him up very tenderly, and put him in a pill-box by himself, with a nice shoot or two of sallow, and stow the box away in your safest pocket, for he will one day be a purple emperor. I'm afraid you won't have to bring that box out again to-day, but you may inscribe ' iris ' on the lid. It always looks well to have that name on a box, and besides, it just *may* have to come out again. I had one day of blessed memory, when I had gone out on purpose to try for them. I got one off the first bush, and shouted for joy. That was about ten

o'clock.   I went on steadily at sallows till one, my hands
getting sorer and sorer, with a blister here and there, for
a day's beating tries the hardness of your hands as much
as a good row, or an hour's batting, and my temper
becoming more and more ragged, for the day was warm,
and I almost hated the smell of the pines, which is generally
so delicious.   I got a fine assortment of other caterpillars ;
young oak eggars ; cratægi, a cousin of theirs (not the
black-veined white) ; gracilis, and a lot of other common
things, that I did not want much, but no more iris.   I
was getting hungry and thirsty, so I pulled out my lunch,
rather despondently, and my flask, the sight of which
cheered me up a bit.   Then I looked for a place in the
shade, where there were no ants, to sit down, and the
best place seemed close to a tiny sallow bush about a
foot high—a scrubby little beast of a tree.   It hardly
looked worth beating, but I screwed up my exhausted
energy, and smote it, and got iris number two.   Lunch
after that was a very different affair.   In fact, I'm afraid
I rather hurried over it, for I felt sure that there was iris
in every bush.   I quite forgot those three dull hours.
However I soon had cause to remember them, for I went
on and on smacking away at a lot of likely looking bushes
and getting nothing but more blisters, and a lot of common
things, boxes and boxes of them.   At last my right hand
was so blistered, that I had to wrap a handkerchief round
it, and I was so hot and weary, that I was glad to undress,
and wallow like a pig in a little pool, not much bigger
than a bath, and only half as deep, full of water-beetles
and things, and to dry on the handkerchief off my blistered
hand, helped by the sun and tiny breeze.   But my reward
was to come.   I was nearly worn out, but the freshness
of the bath lasted me for another half-hour, and just as
I had made up my mind to give in, I saw a lean sallow,
right out in the open, with only three lanky boughs on

it. I held them over my tray in turn, and smacked as hard as my hand would let me, and off the very last branch I got one, two, and even three real live iris caterpillars, making five for the day. I never thought of going on for more. I couldn't have beaten another branch. But I sat and gloated over them for nearly half-an-hour, and then limped off home, worn out, but vastly contented. Don't you think it was worth a day's grind ? Just fancy ! Five purple emperors in one day. Many are the days since that, when I have beaten all day, and taken none, or only one ; so you need not come to live in Hampshire on the supposition that you can go out just when you like in May, and take in caterpillars of iris.

Those same sallows, in autumn, will give you cater-pillars of the sallow kitten, a cousin of the puss moth ; ziczac, one of the so-called prominents ; the eyed hawk moth ; and very likely the poplar hawk moth ; and a lot of nice Geometers, pretty little fellows with a loop in the middle of them, all of which spend the winter as chrysalises. Out of the birches you will get, in the spring, caterpillars of roboraria, the largest of the Geometers, and papilionaria, the great green emerald, and various others ; and in the autumn, dromedarius, another of the prominents, who also lives in the alders, as does papilionaria. The oaks will give you a whole host of things too long to mention ; but beware of a green beast called trapezina, and a dark-brown beast called satellitia ; they are both cannibals, and you'll soon learn to recognise them, because you'll catch them devouring their neighbours, in a leisurely and business-like way, in your flower-pots ; and I have seen trapezina rush at the nearest victim, and start a meal, even in the beating-tray. I've got a bred series of each of these in my collection, and shudder to think how many devoured caterpillars each specimen represents. The beeches in the autumn

H

will produce *coryli*, a pretty light-brown caterpillar, and, if you have luck, the lobster moth. Don't run away and howl, if you see in the tray an extraordinary-looking beast like a cross between a brown scorpion and a lobster. He's only a caterpillar, and rather a rare one. I once had a bag full of sixty, from a lucky capture of a female moth on a beech trunk in June. They began life rather

like ants, and I used them to frighten my lady friends, who wanted to poke my caterpillars with the end of their parasols. When I showed them these, they never wanted to see any more. There is one more tree that you ought to beat, though no one would think of caterpillars eating it, and that is the Scotch fir. There is a very nice brown Geometer, called *fasciaria*, in April and May, and several others at the same time, specially the rather rare *abietaria*, and in June a very pretty Noctua, called piniperda, much loved by ichneumon flies. Ten out of every twelve die, I should say : but as one can get them in buckets almost, it doesn't much matter. You are almost sure to beat out a female of this moth into your tray in April, and then you can breed them from the egg. I think that will give you a fair idea of how to go beating. There are common things also to be beaten out of the ordinary hedgerows, especially detached bushes, and I ought to mention also the buckthorn, if you know it, for the brimstone butterfly and a biggish Geometer called rhamnata, both towards the end of May and in June ; and, when you beat the oaks in the autumn, remember that the caterpillars are very fond of the little clusters of short twigs that come out of the main trunk of the tree, and beat them carefully.

Sweeping won't take me long, because you can do it on any grassy bank in April or May, for Noctuæ caterpillars in the evening. The only special things to sweep are the young clusters of sedges by the river-side, also in the evening, for the various members of the wainscot family ; the clumps of nettles, for the burnished brass, and its cousin festucæ, and the golden Y ; and the heather in June, for agathina and neglecta. This latter is pretty work in the New Forest, but tiring to the arms and wrists. You wade in the deep heather, among the young firs, up sheltered slopes, for the latter of the two, swinging your net backwards and forwards, and sitting down on the soft cushions of heather now and then, to inspect the contents by the aid of a lantern, bringing out a handful of heather-tops, ladybirds, beetles, perhaps a sleepy bee which may or may not sting, and here and there a green naked caterpillar, and then, as the evening mists creep up out of the hollows, you climb higher up to where the shorter bell-heather grows on the hill-tops, and sweep

away for agathina automatically and rather wearily, and
watch the mists fill the hollows, till you seem to be standing
on an island in a lonely lake, with perhaps a pony for
company.   And when you have strolled home, and eaten
your bread and cheese, it is well to put agathina each in
his own pill-box, for they are not above suspicion in the
way of cannibalism.   It isn't a long task, for they are
scarce, and a dozen will be a pretty good bag.   And if
you have to bowl in a match next day, you will know,
for the first over or two, that you spent yesterday evening
sweeping the heather.

Perhaps the most interesting thing of all is what I am
now going to introduce to your notice, and that is a
search party, with no appliances but your own naked
eyes, and perhaps a lantern.   Here again, I must rather
mix up the various seasons, but I'll keep you straight as
far as I can.   Come first to that row of old willows, and
pull off a bit of loose bark.   (This is in May.)   You are
pretty sure to find woodlice and earwigs, but curiously
enough, along with them, and unharmed by them, there
will be caterpillars of a Noctua called upsilon.   They
feed on the leaves of the willow at night, and in the daytime hide under the loose bark, especially near the root
of the tree, squeezing themselves into very tight quarters
sometimes, so that you must be careful not to squash
them in pulling off the bark : and hold your hand underneath as you pull it off, or they will tumble out into the
nettles and grass, and you will lose them.   Later on, in
July, if you climb up to the crown of the tree, you will
very likely find, among the old black decayed stuff in
the hollow at the top, chrysalises of nupta, the splendid
crimson underwing, which also live on the willows,
though I have never yet found where the caterpillars go
in the daytime.   And remember that the more you poke
about in funny places, and the more you watch the ways

and habits of your own tame caterpillars, the more you will learn where you are likely to find things. When you put these upsilon caterpillars into a pot with sprays of willow, and proceed to feed them next morning, you will be amazed to find the pot apparently empty, but if you rake away carefully the loose soil round the edge, you will find that they have all hidden themselves about an inch underground : therefore always give them their fresh food in the evening and not in the morning, for they never come to it till night, and tie the pot very tight, or they will squeeze out under the string. They turn to chrysalises just underground, and the moth comes out in July.

Now it is nearly the end of May, and you may come to a lane where the blackthorn grows up in little stunted patches, a yard or two out from the hedge. If it's a sunny day, we may find the splendid great woolly caterpillars of the lappet moth, like a very big oak eggar, basking on a stem, but they generally feed at night, and go down to the bottom of the main stem, among the long grass, in the daytime. So, if you don't see any basking, search at the bottom of the stem, pushing the grass aside, and you will very likely get one or two. They have curious little pimples on them, just like the blackthorn stems, and are splendid great beasts to keep, feeding on hawthorn as well as blackthorn, and, like the oak eggars, they love willow. I generally come for them with a lantern at night, when they are feeding right at the top of the bush, and can't well be overlooked, and you will find, at the same time, the light-brown naked caterpillars of the common small yellow underwing, with a few of the large broad-bordered yellow underwing, also on the sprays of the blackthorn. In this same lane, at the end of September, or in the early days of October, on the trailing sprays of bramble, you can hardly fail to see the bright-brown caterpillars of batis, the peach-blossom moth, perhaps the most beautiful of all the moths : its great rival to my mind being its cousin and companion, derasa, whose dull mud-coloured caterpillars you may find at the same time, though they are much less conspicuous. Batis you can hardly miss : it absolutely shines in the light of the lantern, and as it has a pure white spot on each side of its head, you cannot very well mistake it for anything else, as it sits extended at full length along one of the trailers of bramble.

As we have got into autumn we may as well stay there and go on into the woods where the moss grows up from the ground on to the trunks of the oaks and ashes. On the oaks I'm afraid you'll have to pull it off, because of the crinkly bark. This rather spoils the tree for next year. Under the moss, in a tiny flimsy cocoon, like a bit of white spider's web, are the little red chrysalises of rubricollis, the red-necked footman, which you must keep on damp moss, till next spring, and, besides these, various other chrysalises are to be found, generally in cocoons among the moss, which you will have to pull carefully to pieces, bit by bit ; the best of them being a pretty green Noctua called ridens, which comes out next March. You ought not to go for these till the beginning of November, as rubricollis is very late in turning, being independent of the leaves, as it feeds on lichens on the trunk. After you have had a good spell at the oaks, turn to the ashes. Here you need not strip the moss. There is a nice Noctua, rather like ridens, called ligustri, which spins a small hard black cocoon among the moss. This, as the trunk is fairly smooth, you ought to be able to feel, by pressing your finger-tips gently over the moss, but if you can't feel it, you must strip off the moss, as you did off the oaks. This caterpillar is also very fond of spinning its cocoon against one of the ivy stems, if there are any on the tree. I always expect to get as many by pulling off the ivy, as by seeking among the moss. Only remember that, as you pull it off, sometimes the cocoon is on the ivy, and sometimes on the trunk, where the ivy went, according as it sticks tightest to one or the other, so that you must look in both places. This moth comes out early next June.

We'll go on with the autumn, and transfer our attentions to the sallows. I told you how you could beat out the caterpillars of the sallow kitten in September, but in case you missed them then, you can go for the chrysalises in October and November. All these chrysalises can be got right through the winter, but, as the earwigs, etc., take heavy toll, your chances get obviously smaller as the year goes on. These caterpillars are interesting, in that they always spin their cocoons on the dead wood, so that what would otherwise be a very hard task is made easier. But the cocoons are made so exactly like the wood, that they are very hard to see. The caterpillar gnaws out a hollow along the dead stem, making the pulp into a hard smooth surface, which is just the colour of the wood, and almost on a level with the rest of the surface, often quite level. You will begin by finding one with a hole in it, where an earwig has bored his way in to commit murder. I have never yet trained an earwig to hunt for me. The hole catches your eye. This cocoon you must observe carefully, imagining the hole away, until the look of the thing becomes familiar, and then you will gradually begin to find the untouched ones. It sounds almost impossible, but I have got as many as fifteen in a day, and it is pleasant leisurely work. They are particularly fond of crawling away down the trunk of the tree, and spinning up on some of the dead wood littered about under the tree, so I always begin with that, sitting on the ground, if it is dry enough, and making a pile of all the dead wood as I inspect it, and after that I finger and inspect all the dead wood in the tree. Don't try to take the chrysalis out of the cocoon, but cut off the bit of wood, and keep it in a dry box, and the moth will come out next May. There is also the poplar kitten, which spins an exactly similar cocoon on the trunks of the poplar trees. Here again you will find the empty ones very easily, but the untouched ones are the hardest things to find that you can look for, and even when you find them in the crevices of the bark, as you may now and then, it is no easy matter to get the very thin skinned chrysalis out, without squashing it. The only way is to cut out carefully the very bottom of the cocoon. The chrysalis fits the cocoon like a glove everywhere but there, but when he changed from a caterpillar to a chrysalis, the old caterpillar skin was shoved down to the bottom of the cocoon, so that there is just room to cut enough away to let the chrysalis slide out into your hands, but it is a very delicate operation.

Let us go back to spring for one more instance of how to find caterpillars. This time we'll take the birch trees, for another nice green Noctua called flavicornis. You must have a still day in June, when the leaves are not dancing and flickering, as birch leaves do in a breeze. These caterpillars also feed at night, and you could doubt-less beat them into a tray, with a boy to hold the lantern ; but in the daytime they either fold themselves into a leaf, not rolling it, not taking it head to tail, but side to side always, or else they take two leaves and pull them together, making a snug dwelling-place. The cater-pillar, in its young days, is blackish grey with a red head ; afterwards, a dirty white with a red head. I mention this, because you'll find lots of little wriggling beasts, belonging to the clothes-moths genus, as I call it, and you don't want to breed *them* yet. What you have to do is to stand and gaze at the tree, until a folded leaf, or pair of leaves, catches your eye.   Open this, and see if the caterpillar answers to my description.   Rolled leaves are no good, and you'll find them in hundreds. You won't fail to recognise the real thing, when you get it, especially if they are nearly full grown.   Where you find one, there, be sure, you will find more, so go on moving round and round your tree, inside it and outside it, and fresh leaves will perpetually catch your eye, until either you have got enough caterpillars, or your neck is too stiff to look any more.   These caterpillars come out next March.

I think I have given you instances enough to show you how much there is to learn in the caterpillar world, and I do hope that you will find the study interesting. Books will help you a good deal, but your own power of observation and ingenuity will do more for you than any books.   Of course, if you are only beginning, some of these hints are rather far advanced for you, but you can begin to train your eyes, by going to the poplar trees in July and August, and inspecting the leaves for caterpillars of the puss moth and poplar hawk moth, and in September you can walk along the privet hedges, and pick off the splendid caterpillars of the privet hawk moth.   The great secret of all caterpillar hunting is not to look for the caterpillars themselves at first, but for the place where they have been feeding.   So, if you see a poplar leaf eaten half away, then begin to look for the caterpillar somewhere near, and when you see long bare twigs among the shoots of a privet hedge, the caterpillar will not be far off.

Before I quite leave the subject of searching, I must just tell you about the caterpillars of my dear sibylla, the white admiral.   They are tiny kids in the autumn, on the honeysuckle, and they make for themselves a winter nest of leaves and bits of leaves, on the trailers, and I have even collected these in the winter. Little tiny houses they are, however, and will easily escape your eye. When spring comes, and the new leaves are budding, they wake up, and begin to feed : you should go for them towards the end of May, or even a bit earlier. When full fed, they are bright green, shading to almost white

near the legs, with red spines, and they cling so tight that you won't beat them into a tray. My description makes them seem conspicuous enough, but you won't find them easily at first. Some of my young friends have got two, while I have got twenty. Here again look for the eaten leaves, and then carry your eye back along the stem, and you'll find them asleep after their meal. They specially frequent the low growth of the honeysuckle, round the bottom of the trunks of the oak trees, and you can sit down, and search each tree at your leisure, so it is pleasant and restful work, and you may at the same time find the extraordinary crumpled-up caterpillar of the beautiful lilac thorn, syringaria, with two spikes on his back, just where he humps himself nearly double. He doesn't look a bit like a caterpillar, but you may find him : he always begins to eat a leaf at the very bottom, while sibylla starts at the side.

Now, on looking over these yarns, it rather strikes me that you *may* be so differently situated, that you have no chance of finding many of the caterpillars which I have mentioned. The difficulty is almost unavoidable. I have told you about mine, which I have mostly discovered for myself, and you must discover yours. But, of course, if you never see a white admiral butterfly in your woods, there will be no caterpillars, so you need not worry to look for them. Sugar your trees, and find out what moths live in your country. Keep eggs, and see what the caterpillars do in captivity. And then you will get some idea of what to look for, and where to look for it. A good book will describe the caterpillars, and give you the food-plant, but they don't often tell you all about the inner secrets of its domestic life. These it is your business to find out for yourself, and you ought to jot down in a notebook every single detail that you can notice. It is a good habit to put down observations on paper for future use.

Now let me give you a word or two of advice on the subject of digging for chrysalises in the autumn, a branch of the study which makes a very pleasant variety in its way, but is neither very interesting nor very instructive as compared with the getting and keeping of caterpillars ; for this reason, that you get the insect in its semi-inanimate stage, and there is nothing to do but keep it cool and a trifle damp, with plenty of air : nor is there any great variety in the method to be pursued, though from the point of view of mere collecting, the practice is profitable enough. September and October are the best months, before the mice and beetles and other enemies have reaped too large a share of the harvest. All that you have to do is to dig with a small trowel close round the trunk of trees, especially those standing a little by themselves out in the open, to a depth of about three inches. Oaks, elms, and limes are the best trees to operate on, and perhaps poplars. Under the oaks you will get, amongst others, the very striking green and white Noctua, aprilina, whose grey caterpillars you may also find in the crevices of the bark in June and July. The elms and limes will give you most of the Tæniocampidæ, and also the beautiful lime hawk moth. These latter are almost commoner under the elms than under the limes, and I have got sometimes over a dozen in a couple of hours. The poplars are only useful for the poplar hawk moth. I have no special hints to give you, except to dig carefully, and search the earth carefully, and put the earth back, partly because it is untidy to leave it littered about, and partly because one year's digging makes the soil looser and easier for the next year. I often dug up the earth round a few pet trees in July, so as to make it more comfortable for the caterpillars to bury in later on. I never found the process very interesting, only rather profitable, as you will often get as many as sixty chrysalises of various sorts in a day.

No one can collect and study caterpillars without being amazed at the extraordinary and inexplicable resemblance to their food-plant. I say inexplicable advisedly, for it is so far utterly inexplicable by any working of natural laws. To take one instance. Papilionaria, the big emerald, has caterpillars which feed on the alder and birch. These hatch in the autumn, and hibernate as small caterpillars. In the winter and early spring they are a dull red, and the exact shape of the birch twigs or alder twigs. When the young leaves begin to break, the caterpillar gets a green crest, but, in the case of those that feed on the alder, the tail end remains red, while those that feed on birch get the green right down to the tail, to correspond more exactly to the quicker-opening birch leaves. The next change, when the leaves are full out, leaves them green all over. This may sound a fable, but I'll take anyone who knows nothing of caterpillars, and defy him to pick out of the beating tray the red caterpillars, in early spring, from among the bits of red twigs, and the red and green caterpillars from among the half-emerged leaf-buds. And no amount of natural selection will explain this. One could multiply instances innumerable—the easier task would be to name the exceptions. It must suffice that I mention one or two. Lichenaria is so like a bit of lichen, that I am sure I seldom pick all out of my tray that are in it. Vernaria falls into the tray quite rigid, drab to match the dead scraps of clematis in autumn, and green in spring, with a head chipped off in exact resemblance of the broken pieces. But it is useless to multiply examples. Down to the minutest details they mimic their surroundings, explain it who may. It only adds one more charm to a pursuit, already engrossing enough. And if you are at present untouched by this charm, I can only say " Try it," and if you are only a beginner, as many of you doubtless are, let me advise you to " go deep " ; search right into the inner secrets, and you will never regret it.

CHAPTER VI

ALL KINDS OF PETS

TALKING of caterpillars leads us naturally to talk of pets —of other pets of many kinds, if you are the sort of folk that I look for boys of my acquaintance to be ; for I am very inclined to measure the worth of men and boys by the need they display, or obviously lack, of animal companionship. It is not at all a bad rule to judge of the worth of a man by the way in which he treats dogs, and by the way in which dogs treat him. Not that I want you to limit your pets to dogs and horses ; in fact I have mainly to deal with far different beasts. Dogs and horses want a book to themselves, or ought to come in with hunting and shooting at any rate ; and all my gossip is about humbler, though, I hope, not less interesting things. I have petted many things : I have almost tried to pet most things. I have never got as far as snails or oysters, but it is always rather a reproach to my conscience that I never trained fleas to love me and perform tricks. Anyway they don't love me, and the fact has its compensations and advantages. But if you want to know how far a man can go in the way of making pets, and how amusing very small things can be, you have only to read Mr. Darwin's book about worms, and Sir John Lubbock's delightful book about "Ants, Bees, and Wasps." Those are queer pets, aren't they? But they have been petted, and very successfully petted, by very great men, who will never be accused of being triflers, or of wasting the time that they might have spent on cricket and football.

However, as I say, I never managed to get so far advanced in the study as this, though I knew some spiders very well; not quite so familiarly perhaps as Monsieur, Madame, and Bebé in "Tom Tug" (I hope you have read about them), but still well enough to call on them with an offering of a fly or drone. "Not kind to the fly," did I hear you say? Well! One can't please everybody, and it's no use trying to: the spider was pleased, at all events, and I have made it up by saving many flies from drowning, if not in a butt of malmsey wine, yet in a milk jug. Nature did *rather* put the temptation in my way, I think, when the Michaelmas daisies were out in the garden in October, covered with flies of all colours, and wasps, and red admirals; for there was always a great spider's web somewhere handy, and I got so very tired of watching the fat spotty fellow sitting still in the middle, and he was often so long with nothing to eat, that I felt practically bound to help him to a dinner, particularly as the wasps were so abundant, that there was great difficulty in whisking off a fly without also embracing the very undesirable wasp. And when you had once introduced yourself to his notice in that way, you couldn't very well cut him dead next day, and so it went on, and one's bump of benevolence grew, and led one to look for other worthy recipients of the bounty. I am sorry if you think it was wrong, but I believe I should do it still, if I saw the spider's web handy.

You see, I do so dislike flies.   At any rate, I certainly
got my punishment in the way of including a wasp in
my capture, and he sat down on my hands with great
violence, and you know what that feels like.

I don't quite know which of my pets to introduce
first to you.   Perhaps on the whole Cain ought to come
first, as the person after whom he was called comes earlier
than any of the others.   I'm not quite sure how he got
his name ; I fancy partly because he would have killed
his brother, if he had had a brother handy to kill ; he
was such an irreclaimable savage ; and partly because he
had a mark on his forehead, for he was a badger.   I and
two or three others bought him from his home in
Devonshire for ten bob, which was more than he was
worth in the market, I fancy ; but we got our money's
worth of fun out of him.   He came in a bag, marked
" With great care."   And I'm sure I hope the porters
and guards observed the notice, for Cain was no respecter
of persons, and would as soon have bitten a guard,
dignified or otherwise, as a crossing-sweeper, and when
he bit, he left a mark.

People say that a badger only nips, while an otter
takes the piece out, and I dare say it is true.   No otter
has ever had a piece out of me, and won't now if I can
help it.   All I know is, that when Cain bit, he was like
the old lady in the " Reminiscences of an Irish R.M.,"
his back teeth met, and his front ones therefore went
one better and overlapped, as my dog Sam, if he is still
alive, will swear.   When Cain was at home, he lived in
the Headmaster's stable : I think I may reveal the secret
now without fear of the consequences.   The Headmaster's
groom knew, and found his knowledge worth money,
but the Headmaster didn't.   Our secret nearly got out
once, for Cain got entirely out, and of all silly things to
do, considering that he was not obliged to do it, as we

were, he tried to force his way into a class-room. By great good luck the master who inhabited that particular room was a Devonshire man himself, and recognised a fellow-countryman, and also had the talent for spotting the likely man to have done a particular thing, as we knew to our cost. And all he said was, " Please, So-and-So (naming one of the joint owners), take your cat away from my room." So the situation was saved. We daren't chain Cain, you see, for I don't think it would have been very safe to unchain him, even in his balmies moments. The only way to approach him was by his tail, and that was too short to fasten a chain to. We all got to be great adepts at tailing him. The only thing is, to be very quick about it. Half-measures result in disaster. And you must then hold your arm out stiff, as nearly at right angles to your body as possible. In that position he will curl up, and you will see a flash of white teeth just under your arm, and hear them meet, but if you don't funk it, they will always miss you by a very anxious and uncomfortable inch. If you hang your arm below the perpendicular, ten to one he'll have you by the leg, and if you lift it too high, you swing him inwards and he'll take hold somewhere just under the shoulder, either arm or body ; he's not particular to an inch or two, as long as he can get you somewhere, and teach you not to meddle with a Devonshire man's tail.

For five days in the week Cain lived a peaceful life of uneventful captivity, eating potatoes and bread and milk, and I am bound to say that he had a taste for raw eggs, though I know that, in saying this, I am doing his relations a bad turn. The truth will out eventually, and besides I owe him one for taking a piece out of my breeches. He didn't mean to. He meant, if expression goes for anything, to perforate my leg ; but I pulled him away just in time, and the breeches were rather old, and so

the piece came away.   He never got very tame, though
he always took to his wittles.   We made many advances,
and he was always ready to meet our advances more
than half-way.   But there was always a look in his eye
which prevented the advances from actually meeting,
except when we got him by the tail, while another occupied
his attention as a safe distance in front.   This not very
cordial meeting happened twice a week, unless we got
an extra half-holiday, in which case relations were strained
three times.   On these occasions, Cain was put into a
bag, and taken away on to the downs for a run, with a
very select field of six of us and Sam, a beagle-marked
big terrier—a man of peace by nature, with a liking for
the society of babies and bones—but if there was one
thing he couldn't stand, it was Cain ; and if there was
a man in the world, whom Cain wished to annihilate, it
was that identical Sam.   The results of this emnity were
twofold : firstly, that Sam had to run in a leash, or we
should have had no run at all : it would have been all
wrath, and malice, and bloodshed ; and secondly, that
when Cain got too near rabbit holes, or sulked in a big
clump of brambles, blood *was* shed ; not the blood of
one, but the blood of both.   In this way they got in
several very enjoyable spaces of two minutes, which was
about the time it took us to persuade them to leave hold
of one another.   They must have bitten very clean.
We never exactly inspected Cain's mouth, as it wasn't
easy : at least, it was, but we didn't much want to.   But
Sam healed in a day, and Cain could eat potatoes in half-
an-hour.   Towards the end of their acquaintance, their
animosity abated, or else they considered that they had
each proved the other's valour sufficiently.   At any rate,
if Cain refused to stop and skirmish around, till we could
get up, Sam learnt how to take him by the ear, and keep
out of the way of his teeth, and also, owing to good

living, Cain got less handy at turning round sharp. But, in the early days of his activity, what runs we had ! I'll never forget one, where he went in a bee-line for the river, and swam that mighty stream, and two good-sized tributaries. It suited us of course exactly, and we went through too, Samuel swimming by our side. About two fields farther, an old man was digging, and Cain took him into his line. The old fellow was undeniably old, but he had apparently never seen a badger, and he didn't like the look of Cain, nor perhaps of the rest of the hunt, for there had been a good deal of mud in the last of the tributaries. He left his spade, and the pace he made for the hedge was, for a very old man, distinctly good : we had no time to go and offer him our congratulations, for Cain was gaining on us rather in our wet things. He eventually got to ground in a drain-pipe under a gateway, which was too small for Sam's figure, so we had to get some straw from a rick, as time was pressing, and smoke him out. I never saw him come out from anywhere with a worse expression on his face. Even Sam turned his head away. However, he was tailed and taken home. Not long after this—and I always suspect that elderly man of having borne malice—we received an anonymous intimation, that unless our runs ceased, information would be given in high quarters ; and as our characters for high moral virtue were rather precious at the time, we did not think it well to disregard the warning, for the style of the letter looked as if the writer was in earnest. So we took advantage of an opportune holiday to take Cain and Samuel down to the New Forest, where, after a final run among the heather, and one little parting fracas with Sam, he was dismissed with our blessing, and the hopes that he would soon find a nice wife, and be the father of a great nation. He had a great influence on Sam's future, for soon afterwards it became necessary for that sagacious hound to change masters. Unforeseen circumstances arose, and the world is very full of meddlesome busybodies, who mind everyone's business rather than their own. So I gave him to a sporting pork-butcher, who had a place in the very select circle of my acquaintances. And when I asked after his welfare later on, I was told that he was worth his weight in gold. Now his weight, when he and I parted company, was no trifle, so I was very interested, and asked for the reason of this astounding fact. And I found out that Sam's master and Sam had been bringing a lively young pig from market in a cart one day, and that piggy had effected a sensational escape from the vehicle, and started off home at a brisk pace, too brisk a pace for my friend, who was losing his figure, to put it politely. But Samuel thought, when he glimpsed the flying animal, that Cain had come back once more, and was off like an arrow. Mindful of the lessons which he had learnt in the days of his warfare, he went for the ear, and held manfully to his squealing captive, till his panting and irate master arrived on the scene and completed the capture. Hence that enthusiastic statement about the gold. I have ceased to hear of Sam, but I am afraid that time must have prevailed against him. Peace to his ashes! I should never be surprised to see the ghost of him and Cain in deadly combat on the downs.

The mention of piggy leads me naturally to say a brief word about Pluto. Why "Pluto," I don't remember, unless it was because he kept his sty so dirty that he was "king of the infernal regions." But it is not of his home life that I wish to speak, nor of his glorious transformation into sausages and brawn, but of his walks abroad. He was allowed out in the summer in the pasture, with the cow, whose name, if I remember right, was Mrs. Doodles, and with Toby the pony, and it struck

me one day that he might be used as a mount, so I lured
him to me with a vegetable of sorts, and, after perfidiously
scratching his back, I threw a leg over and was astride,
holding on to his ears for all I was worth. He gave
one snort of terror or indignation, and careered round
the field. His action was rather short and cramped, but
the novelty made it most exhilarating, and I may fairly
say that I thoroughly enjoyed my ride. Many writers
have written on the joys of riding *after* pig, but I rather
fancy I am the first to bring into public notice the delights
of riding *on* pig. Of course my ride became an important
part of my daily programme, for the excitement never
lessened, since Pluto became very wary and cunning.
He had three great resources. He never kicked, or
bucked, or reared. But the field had at any rate two
sides and a pond. One side was rough palings, and
another side was a hedge overhanging a wide ditch.
The pond explains itself: Pluto generally went straight
for it and into it, and I had to slip off behind just before
he got there. But sometimes he took the palings on
the way, and jammed my leg against them, and the hedge
was his last discovery, and took me unawares, and I
found all the prickles full in my face, and my mount
gone to ground in the most unorthodox way, before I
realised that there was room for Pluto under the hedge
and not for me. Let no one say in my hearing that pigs
lack intelligence. The only thing was to catch the beast
as far away from these obstacles as possible, and get as
long a ride as circumstances permitted, and slip off his
curly tail, for when he once reached home in the pond,
or under the hedge, he refused to budge, and only winked
the other eye when I offered carrots. In due time he
became bacon, and I thought that the exercise in the
summer months had improved the quality. But life was
dull when he left the pasture : I did conceive the idea of

riding Mrs. Doodles, and found her once near enough
to the palings to jump on to her humpy and angular
back, and get fairly astride.   She began to kick at once
viciously, and it was very painful, but I was still there.
When she started to run, however, I was extraordinarily
glad to roll off on to the soft grass, and never since that
day have I ridden cow, nor can I think that anyone could
find either pleasure or excitement in it, only an over-
whelming and predominating pain.   But try it, if you
like : you may be differently constituted.   Have some
soft ground handy, that's all.

Perhaps the commonest and best loved of all a boy's
pets are birds of various kinds : and I was no exception
in this matter.   In fact I have kept so many that it is
rather difficult to know where to begin.   But far the
best beloved was my kestrel hawk.   I have kept many
more than one, but only one became ever really tame,
nor do I know now why this particular one so far excelled
all the others.   I got them all equally young, and treated
them very much in the same way ; but the others only
tolerated my presence : they would sit on my hand of
course, when there was food to be had ; but they never
showed any real desire to make friends for friendship's
sake, like this particular one did.   He never had a name,
strangely enough.   I don't fancy I could have ever found
the right one.   He had no special peculiarities to lay
hold of except his extraordinary devotion to me.   Now
I am rather glad, for it gives him a kind of distinction
in my memory.   Of course the friendship ripened
gradually, as most really strong friendships do.   Have
you ever liked for long a person who took you by storm
all in a moment ?   I don't think I ever have.   I know
I've disliked uncommonly some persons who seemed
wonderfully pleasant at first.   I was keeping two other
hawks in the same cage, a big box standing on its side,

with bars nailed down the front. I never liked wire ; they catch their legs and wings in it somehow. And *he* gradually began to attract my notice, till one day he fairly startled me by rubbing his head against my hand of his own free-will, and by obviously wanting to be petted. He got plenty of it after that, you may be sure ; till at last, when his wings grew, I did not cut them, as I did the others, but let him learn to fly, cautiously at first, but soon more freely ; and in the end he only went to bed once or twice a day, just when I was in school. As long as I was out and about, he was somewhere handy, generally hunting for beetles, when he was not sitting on my hand or shoulder. His great joy was to be tickled at the back of the head, like most birds, and under the wing, which many birds resent, as an unwarrantable liberty. And he would lie on his side with one wing half raised, waiting for it. Poor old man ! His end was more tragic than that of most bird pets. They generally either die in their beds, or escape. But he and I were pottering about one day rather idly, when there was a cry of " Heads." I jumped out of the way instinctively, and the cricket-ball fell full on my poor kestrel, and slew him on the spot. Whether I took any sudden vengeance on any one, I can't say. It was not unlikely. But I hope now that my grief was too deep. That is the one great disadvantage of really loving your pets, for when all is said and done, they lead a precarious existence, and when they die they leave such a blank. I'm bound to say, it soon gets filled up again in a way. But it occurs so often, that I sometimes really wonder whether the man who never has any pets isn't on the whole happier. However, it's not any manner of use discussing that question, for the simple reason that I can't do without them in some form or other, nor do I expect that you can either. Therefore let us go on loving them as much as we can, for you ought never to keep them, unless you are prepared to make some sacrifice of your own convenience for their comfort. A man has no business to keep a dog, if he can't give it exercise. The dog may be happy enough, and well enough treated, but it will get unhealthy, and want to be always scratching in consequence. And then it will grow fat and smelly, and live only for its food, until it finally ceases to be a dog, in the proper sense of the word.

I did not mean, when I began this chapter, to talk about dogs at all, but I seem to have got drawn into it, as I was almost bound to be. Anyway I can't tell you the names, nor sketch the characters, of all the dogs that have lived with me. So many people have written on this subject, and the joys of reading about " Tom Tug " are so great, as to make it rash for me to think of doing more than give you just a word or two of advice. But perhaps I may do that much, without being stale and unprofitable. Dogs and boys go so much together in every household, that whether the boy is the real owner or not, he has a great deal to do with the making or marring of the dog's character. And I have seen a great many boys in a fair way towards ruining the dogs with whom they have to deal, and incidentally I may remark, doing their own little selves no very great good in the process. For if it be true that you may judge the master from his dog, as many people say, it is also pretty true that you may make a shrewd guess as to what a boy will grow up like, from the way in which you see him training a dog. Some boys, for instance, are never happy unless they are trying to get a dog to make a fool of himself, either in the way of losing his temper, or pulling handkerchiefs to pieces, or digging holes in the garden for imaginary rats. I know it's attractive, in a way ; but people don't like the man who is always getting his fellows to display their weak points, instead of their good ones ; and that's what you'll grow up into, if you don't mind. However, I mustn't preach. Let me say that there are at least three great rules to observe in dealing with a dog. (i) *Never be impatient :* tell him the same thing over and over again, and insist time after time, quietly and gently, on his doing it. It is rather wearisome, but pays in the end. (ii) *Don't let him rule you.* When you call him, make him come to you, however long it takes, and don't give in and go to him. Don't give him scraps whenever he asks for them. Don't let him cadge round the table. If he may come into the room make him sit in one place, wherever it is. Don't let him sit on the chairs. The floor is good enough. But if he must have a chair, let him have one only, and teach him to know it wherever it may stand. This is quite easy. And let it stand near a window, as a rule : dogs like to see what is going on outside. (iii) *Don't rule him too hard.* Dogs have individuality, which ought to be encouraged. Keepers are generally splendid breakers of dogs, but they break them too much to one pattern, and the dog is liable to become a machine. I like a dog to learn to go his own way, within certain definite limits, and unless a dog is kept for a certain definite purpose, like pointing or retrieving—in which case he ought to do very little else—I always encourage any tricks or peculiarities, unless they are a nuisance. Above all things be consistent. Don't let a dog do a thing one day, and then, because you are out of temper, punish him for doing it the next day. I saw a boy one day flicking an old glove about a puppy's head, and encouraging him to catch hold and pull : a while after, he found one of his own batting-gloves mauled about, with obvious marks of teeth on it. And then you should have heard him squeal, " Where's that beastly puppy ? give me a stick, and I'll

teach him to pull my gloves about." That's the sort of
thing you have to be so very careful not to do. And
if you keep pups, you must be absolutely prepared for
trouble; they *will* worry things, and dig in the garden,
and no amount of licking will stop them. Very few
pups want more than two good smackings, one to teach
them that it is pleasanter not to be smacked, and another
to warn them that it can happen more than once, and
they ought to get it hot enough not to want another,
or they will disregard your orders barefacedly. After
that patience, and an occasional tap will produce a very
orderly and well-regulated and intelligent dog.

Some time ago I began to talk about bird pets, and
got called away. I'm sorry. I was saying that all boys
liked them. Jackdaws are as good birds as any to keep,
but you ought always to have two. They are very sociable
birds, and thrive better in pairs, and the way they talk
to one another is delicious. And, I forgot to tell you,
don't cut any bird's wing. All the quill feathers have
a broad side and a narrow side. Strip the broad side of
two out of every three, and you'll prevent their flying,
and yet won't spoil the look of the wing at all. I always
think a cut wing looks worse on a jackdaw than on any
other bird. I don't recommend owls: I had a fine
couple of long-eared owls once, which I got out of a
nest of four in March (they must have started early)
nearly full fledged. Savage little beasts they were, as
bad as a sparrow-hawk, and that's saying a good deal:
all claws, and very long and sharp claws too. People
talk about " cruel curved beaks," but it is the claws that
do the mischief. I kept these owls on fresh food for a
month by throwing stones. But they never approached
tameness. They were half asleep all day, and squealed
all night worse than cats, so that I was rather glad when
they broke their way out one night. I always think

that they were helped from outside by other owls. There were marks of claws all over the cage bars, and unless the two determined to wreak vengeance on their prison-house after they made their escape, there must have been a bird outside to make some of the marks. It is interesting either way. My experience of the views of other birds towards birds in cages all goes to prove that they do take a great interest in them. Too much, sometimes. Black-birds and thrushes will inevitably poison their young ones, if you take a nest of nearly fledged ones, and cage them out for the old ones to feed them. It happened to me so regularly, that I gave up the habit, and fed them myself, and reared them easily enough. I saw the old birds feed them on something, and never could make out what it was. It was always fatal after about a day. It is a very pleasant thing to take and hand-feed the bulk of the young birds in your garden. Chopped egg rolled in oatmeal, with plenty of green food, and afterwards the ordinary canary mixture that you buy, is what seemed to me to suit them best. I very seldom lost any, and after you have had them for about a month, you let them go, and for a long time afterwards they will come to your call, and feed round about your feet, scrambling all round you for the food, while the envious sparrows sit at a safe distance. I really believe that a considerable part of the pleasure came from scoring off the sparrows. Not that I don't love the impudent little scoundrels in a way, just as one loves a little street-boy, whose one idea is to be a nuisance, to the outward eye at any rate. I have never, however, detected any trace of the finer and softer feelings in the sparrow's breast. When without ceremony I pull their nests out of my ivy to save my garden, and particularly my yellow crocuses, their whole attitude and bearing is jaunty and cheerful, and suggests the idea that they are saying to their respective mates,

"Well! thank goodness those troublesome brats are
gone." And if you don't burn the nests, they are all
up in the ivy again in a couple of days. I cannot really
like people who won't take a snub, and cannot see that
their presence is disliked. So it was a real pleasure to
me when the finches and thrushes got all the food. My
only sorrow was that I could never get them to perch
on my shoulder, or even on my hand. If I put my hand
very quietly on the ground, they would scramble over it,
but they always jumped off in a great hurry, when they
felt their feet touch the warm flesh. I think you might
try to rear a few of your garden birds : one or two may
die in the process, but if you find that many do, give up
trying it. They are so easy, granted care and trouble on
your part, that if you fail, it must prove that you are not
fitted for the task, but you will lose a great pleasure.

My one sparrow-hawk lived long enough to escape,
and take to chicken-killing in the next farm-yard, and
get shot for his pains by an irate farmer. But I cannot
honestly say that he was a success. He never once let
me come near him without throwing himself on his back,
and sticking out a remarkably vicious claw, and screaming
as if he was being murdered; but when I threw him a
dead sparrow he lost no time in pulling it to pieces. He
was a great failure as a pet, though he grew into a very
fine and handsome bird. Nor did I do much better with
a couple of young lapwings, whom I was much drawn
towards, because their legs were like mine, very long
and very thin, and their disposition was modest and
retiring (also like mine, I trust), so much so that their
one idea was to squat and hide themselves. I found
that they were going to die in captivity, so I wired in
a bit of garden and they recovered, and so far got tame
as to come for worms, when I threw them from a considerable distance. But the cat got one, and showed

such an obvious determination to have the other, in spite
of my managing to put a bucket of water well over her
as she was watching it, that I thought it kinder to take
him out into the wilds, where the other lapwings lived,
and let him go, but I doubt whether he knew how to
get worms for himself, never having had a mother, so
to speak. He may have been one of those that I shot
next winter, for all I know. Funny fellows, aren't we ?
Pet a thing one moment, and shoot it the next. Just
like my dog Mike and his cat, kiss it first and try to worry
it afterwards. That pretty nearly brings me to the end
of my bird pets. But there are one or two other favourites
I mustn't forget. I kept, besides those that I have
mentioned, magpies and gulls, but have nothing very
special to tell you about them, and one very hard winter,
I had a whole attic full of birds, including two rooks,
for nearly a month, who all got pretty tame, and did
not fight a great deal, though Mr. and Mrs. Rook were
inclined to think that the whole place belonged to them.
Luckily I had no jackdaw, or there must have been trouble.

I come now to the major and minor convolvulus.
I was rather proud of the name. I wonder if you could
possibly guess what they were. Two grass snakes. I
caught them both on the same day, and did not at all
admire the kind of scent they used, but I tied them up
in my best pocket handkerchief, and brought them home.
I wonder what the washerwoman thought about that
handkerchief. Mine were never particularly presentable
objects when they reached her hands, but that one was
particularly unsavoury. The minor reptile soon learnt
to give up scent, and was speedily transferred to my
pocket, where he lived till I got tired of him and let him
go, living mainly on bread and milk. But his major
brother, or aunt, was never fit for close companionship,
and had to live in a box, and only came out for a walk

now and then.   He, or she, did not seem to require
much exercise, being generally engaged in digesting a
frog.   I never could manage to see him take his food.
I didn't exactly want to, because some people say that
the poor food is sucked down all alive, hind-legs first,
and it doesn't sound a pleasant thing to watch ; and yet
in a way I was most anxious to see the process, on the
principle of wanting to see everything that one's pets
did.   But I never got a chance.   Major would let the
frog hop over him and almost sit on his head.   He always
had a kind of look in his evil eye, as much as to
say, " Wait till that beggar's gone, and then I'll teach
you how to hop ! " but he always waited, and when I
went again there was seldom any frog, only a big bulge
about the major's middle.   I had quite an exciting tragedy
with a later snake.   I had caught a biggish mouse alive
in a trap, and thought that my snake might like a change
of diet, so I got a deep box, and put in first the snake
and then the mouse.   There was a momentary scramble
and a hiss, and then the snake coiled up on one side of
the box, while the mouse sat in a corner with all his bristles
up.   But he did not wait for long.   I could not have
believed it if I had not seen it.   He came to the speedy
conclusion that the snake was afraid, and went for him
like a streak of lightning, and had him by the back of
the neck with his teeth deep in, before either I, or I believe
the snake, realised what was happening.   I don't think it
was in a boy's nature to spoil a fight ; anyway I didn't,
and in about four rounds the snake was as dead as a
snake ever seems to be, with his head nearly bitten off.
That mouse had a large lump of cheese, and he was so
hungry after his battle, that he began on it almost at
once.   In the evening he was dismissed into a corn-stack
in the fields, as being the safest place for so bold a warrior,
and I hope that he escaped all the dangers to which a

mouse is liable. He had nothing to fear from snakes at all events. I wonder if you find it funny how the name of a pet suddenly jumps into your head, while others never get a name. Directly I got those two snakes, I knew what their names were. One friend of mine never gave his pets less than four names each, chosen apparently at random ; and yet he never forgot them, or gave them to the wrong pet, and as soon as ever he got a new pet he seemed to produce four names, and he always employed them all. Until I got used to it, I howled with laughter, when I heard him gravely address one of his jackdaws as Martin Luther, Sam Weller, or some such appalling mixture. His view was that you couldn't reasonably expect an animal to behave well, unless it had a fair lot of respectable names. He certainly did produce the most extraordinarily solemn lot of pets you ever saw. His jackdaws were different birds to my rowdy rascals, and refused to associate with them. I suppose the burden of their names was too much for them. Whatever you may call them, I don't think you'll care for snakes a great deal, except either as curiosities for a while, or to make yourself a curiosity for a while, both of which views seem to me reasonable. I can safely tell you that you'll not be popular with maiden aunts, which is always unwise, as I hope I have already shown you, nor with sisters, who even if they are not included among your pets, as I hold that they ought to be, have it in their power to make things very uncomfortable for you on various occasions.

Nor are toads much better, though I kept one for a long time, mainly in the hope of seeing him eat a fly or a slug, but I believe that he never touched anything all the while I had him. The only time he displayed any animation was when I pulled his obstinate mouth open, and got my brother to pop in a slug, and push it down with a feather, for fear he should starve.   He did not struggle during the process at all, but when it was over he made a bad face, stretched out his neck like a cock beginning to crow, and spat it out. How can you get on with a fellow, who will neither eat for himself nor allow himself to be fed.   There is no possible interest in trying to tame either toads or snakes, as far as I can see.   But my hedgehog was a much better fellow, and friendly in his way, though the nature of his coat made it difficult to pet him.   I remember I got into a great row from spreading my handkerchief over him, and trying to persuade my baby brother, who had not begun trousers, that it was a nice cushion.   I should have done it too, had the young beggar not learnt to distrust me, when I seemed particularly friendly.   He got his first lesson, when I caught a tomtit in a brick trap, and offered it to him to kiss.   Tomtits are very ready with their beaks, and his young lips were tender.   Of course it was a wicked shame to try and get the poor young beggar to sit on a hedgehog, and I well deserved all I got, and knew I did.   But the idea jumped into my head, and was rather irresistible, and I never could learn to stop and think of the consequences.   I only mention the incident as a warning.   The hedgehog in question loved milk, and when he got tame enough not to curl up when I touched him, as he soon did, he would take black beetles and woodlice (crollywogses, my gardener calls them) out of my fingers, and crunch them up, smacking his lips over them in a way that fairly gave you the shivers.   He lived for a long while in the kitchen, and I don't remember what became of him.   But I must give you a word of warning and tell you a very sad story. Only last year, as my kitchen was very full of beetles, I got a hedgehog, and before she went to bed, the cook opened wide the oven door, to air it, I suppose.   And

sometime in the early morning the poor hedgehog must
have found it, and thought it a nice warm place, and
gone right to the back.   And in the morning—but you
can guess the rest.   We could not make out what the
smell of burning was.   I tell you about it rather un-
willingly, only because it might so very easily happen
again in anyone's kitchen, and lots of people do keep
hedgehogs.

Now, as to the keeping of ferrets.   The picture will
help you.   The hutch stands against the wall, and it is

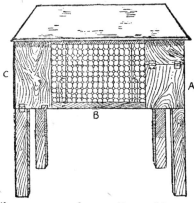

well to nail some sort of tarpaulin or felt on to the roof,
as it does not do to get them wet.   They are not quite
so hardy as they look.   *A* is their bedroom : the bottom
half of the side you see in the picture is fixed, but the
top half swings forward on a couple of hinges.   This
compartment I should fill with wood-shavings, not straw,
or else they'll get covered with ticks.   The middle part,
B, is their run.   I should make the opening to this in
the roof, and just keep a small sprinkling of straw on the
floor.   If you do this, they will always be clean in their
house and go through to *C :* the floor of which you

K

will make mainly of wire-grating, and put no straw in it on any account, or they will never see any difference between their rooms. I should make the whole side of this either swing forward on a hinge, or slide out some-how, as you ought to swill this end well with water every day. It is most important to keep them clean and dry, or they get foot-rot and other maladies. As to the feeding of them, I believe mainly in a diet of bread and milk, with a rat or rabbit thrown into them twice a week: even then don't let them have it for long, just a good tear at it, and then take it away. You can do a good deal, in your methods of feeding them, to teach them not to lie up in a hole. Of course, for rabbits, you will generally muzzle them, but for rats you can't possibly do so, and it is very irritating, when they refuse to come out after killing a rat, as they do sometimes. Some people feed them on nothing but rats or rabbits, giving them next to nothing to drink, and the result is that they are so greedy for blood that when they kill they lie up for a long time. Let them have plenty of bread and milk, and never let them have a rat for long, and I think you will find that they generally come out of the hole quickly. But if they do lie up, and you are in a hurry, take a small bag of straw with you, and leave it open close to the mouth of the hole, and after a while send a boy back, and you will always find your ferret curled up in the bag. The only other thing to be careful of is the young ones, if you breed them. They get " the sweats," on the eleventh day generally after they are born, just before they open their eyes. The name explains the disease : they sweat profusely for some reason, and generally die.

Directly they begin, take out the shavings, and make them a nest of damp green meadow-grass, gathered with the dew on it, if possible, and they will generally come through their trouble all right. That ought to give you some idea of how to keep them, and very amusing pets they are. There is no comparison, to my mind, between them and the silly rabbits and guinea-pigs that some boys keep : and they are infinitely more profitable, if you want to make a little money. You can nearly always get a market for them in the *Exchange and Mart*, or in other ways.

I have about come to the end of my talk about Pets, though I should rather have liked to tell you about my dormice and my aquarium. But there is not very much to tell, as the dormice were mostly asleep, except when they were running races up the blind-cord, stretched tight at a pretty good angle from the window, and the aquarium was always a bit of a sorrow. The great fun was the making of it in the beginning : a bell-glass turned upside down on a big flower-pot, then the bottom well covered with smart pebbles, and a nice bit of weed planted among them, and water up to the brim. Then to the brook for sticklebacks and water-snails and beetles ; and for a day or so there was joy and admiration in the breasts of the Hewett family. But the water-snails crawled out, and got squashed on the carpet, which caused friction, and the beetles often did the same ; if not, there was endless warfare between them and the fishes ; and the fishes also pulled one another to pieces, or burst up from eating too many bread-crumbs. One large beetle was generally the survivor, who was as a rule set at liberty, after he had eaten the final champion and survivor of the sticklebacks. It was all grossly mismanaged, no doubt ; but new sticklebacks and beetles were so easy to get, whenever we felt an ardent desire to make an aquarium, that I am afraid we never took very great trouble with them, our main delight being to watch the warfare. And this seems to lead me to my final remark, and that is, that you have no business, even with beetles and sticklebacks I fear, to keep things just for your own fun, if it is to their sorrow. I know that I have sinned against my own rule at times, but on the whole I have done my best to make my many friends happy, and have gained such happiness myself thereby, that I can honestly say, "Keep pets of all sorts: you'll never regret it: and see that they don't either."

CHAPTER VII

SALT-WATER PURSUITS

Now I'm going to take you for a holiday to the sea. Not that sort of sea where kids in funny attire, or precious little attire, dig holes in the sand, though I have seen quite elderly boys stealthily taking a hand in the game, and enjoying themselves in a sort of frightened way : but the proper wild sea, where you do pretty much what you like, and have a boat and boatman of your own. I never quite make out wherein lies the charm of the sea, as compared with fresh water. I have swum or swimmed (they both look funny words) in a fresh-water lake by moonlight, when the mist was lying on the water, and the plovers were calling about my head, and, as I skirted a reed-bed, the water-hens were clucking and the fish splashing, and there is no doubt it was pure delight. Have you ever read George Macdonald's " Light Princess " ? She induced me to try it, and it was sheer revelry, but it never gave me quite that thrill that a moon-light swim in the sea sends tinkling along the bell wires of my nerves. And I have rowed before breakfast on

another aristocratic pond on a June morning, when all
the earth and water smelt sweet, and chased a flock of
thirty swans, till they rose and flew back over my head,
and all the air was full of the hiss of great white wings,
but it could not compare, for sheer joy and witchery,
with the half-light as the day broke at six o'clock on a
January morning, and I lay flat on the pebble ridges of
the island, where I got the ringed plover's eggs, and
pulled down out of the haze, or failed to do so, the mallard
and sheldrake that came within shot.   There is a wild
and untamed spirit in the ocean that calls to something
primitive in us ; that calls and gets its answer.

I think I can probably excuse my enthusiasm for the
sea best, by trying to sketch for you a few scenes, where
the ocean and I have been intimate friends.   Of course
I had done the usual things in the way of digging sand,
and messing about, from very early days, but one day
came a note from a friend, saying that he was bored,
and tired, and hated everything, and would I come with
him into a lonely place, away from the noisy world ?
I always had the gift of the gods called silence, and could
be with a man all day without saying a word, and that's
why he picked me, I suppose.   So we—or rather he, for
he was the managing partner in the business—took a
little tent, and went down to the sandhills of the
Lincolnshire coast.   Have you ever slept out in the
sandhills ?   I have done it several times since then, and
know now that the main thing is to keep away from the
rabbits, because rabbits keep fleas, and it's all nonsense
to say that rabbits' fleas don't attack the human being,
because I know that they do.   But I did not find it out
on that first memorable expedition, because there were
no rabbits anywhere about.

I found out mainly two things ; that it was very difficult
to know when to go to bed, because the moon was up,

and the sea was lapping almost up to our feet, and we
sat on the hillocks, talking about everything that there
is to talk about, or rather he talked and I listened
sympathetically, and thought how jolly everything was.
And secondly, that when you did at last turn into the
snug little tent, it was very hard to go to sleep. I chose
a nice hollow, with my coat for a pillow, and a rug over
me, and the soft sand below me, and felt very peaceful
and comfortable, but there was a sort of spirit of wake-
fulness about. It was the sea's fault. It would go on
whispering, and I wondered what it was trying to tell
me. I believe now that it was only saying, " Go to
sleep, for I'm here looking after you," but I didn't understand then, and I kept on resting, but always awake.
And at last I crept out, and saw the phosphorus sparkling
on the crests of the waves, and after watching that for
some time, I crawled back, and was asleep directly. We
woke with a jump about seven o'clock, and found the
waves almost at our doors, so we took off our flannels,
and had a bit of a swim, and then went off to the pub to
breakfast. After that we hired a couple of shrimping
nets—things on poles that you push in front of you—
and strolled into the sea in our flannels. We began in
the shallow pools, but soon worked our way into the
big sea. And very jolly it was. I finished the morning
up to my armpits, with the waves swelling against my
cheek, in the brilliant sunshine. It was fine to watch
their crests coming, ruffled by a bit of breeze from the
east, and then feel them half lift you off your feet, and
pass shorewards. Shrimps we got in basketsful, and little
soles, and all sorts of queer things. The crabs were the
funniest ; cheeky little brutes ! when I waded to shore
and emptied the pocket of my net on the sands, every
crab seized the nearest shrimp, and bore him off
triumphantly with one claw aloft in the air, and buried

himself and his prey in the wet sand. I always let them go, because we had shrimps to spare, and I never ceased to laugh at the cheek of the little beggars. It did not seem to enter into their heads (if they have heads) that they were my captives, and therefore liable to death; as far as I could see, their only idea was, " Here's shrimps; let's have one."

There was also a small fish like a perch, with a sharp back-fin, whom by mere luck I did not handle. I found out afterwards that his pretty back-fin could sting, and swell your arm right up to your shoulder. So beware of him when you go shrimping. We fed half the village with our shrimps. Like all people who live near the sea, they seemed extraordinarily pleased with a present of fish. You'd think they could just go and help themselves, but they don't somehow. I suppose they feel bound to sell all they catch. We didn't bother to change —we had only been working in a pair of flannel bags and a flannel shirt—and we just let these dry on us, as we strolled up to the inn to lunch. It sounds rather foolhardy now, but it did us no harm, and I doubt whether, during the whole ten days that I was there, I ever changed a rag. You can't say it was uncleanly, because I was in the sea most of the day. We strolled up the shore in the evening till we were dry, and then dined and went to bed, and bathed in our things in the morning. I know, at the end of the time, that I was just as red as a lobster all over, from the sun and salt water, and I don't think I ever felt fitter in my life, and my companion came back absolutely cured of his fit of the blues. It was very much " reds," and not " blues," with us at the end of our time. We might just as well have been pickled.

So much for my first real trip to the sea. A winter or two afterwards, I went to the same coast to shoot, and found my pub still there, full of tales of the two lunatics, who shrimped all day, and fed and slept on the sand in their wet things. Children pointed the finger of admiration at me, and said " That's him." That old inn smacked of square bottles and smuggling captains, with its low rooms, and great oak beams, and big fire-places, and right comfortable I was. I had a private room, and a weather-beaten gillie always at my beck and call, morning, noon, or night, for the extravagant sum of five shillings a day : there was also a piano in my room— at least it had been a piano ; when it came under my hands, most of the notes sounded the same, but it served very well on one or two great occasions, when I had a party of bearded fishermen to tea, to lead a ramping chorus. The tune didn't matter, because there wasn't one to speak of. The only thing was, to let someone sing a verse, and then get the time of the chorus more or less, and bang hard on the piano. It might have hurt some sensitive ears, but you can get used to most things. I used sometimes to wonder why no nautical song has less than seventeen verses. My own feeble efforts, about " a certain Billy Kidd," seemed very short. But as they were always encored, out of politeness, I fear, they reached a reasonable length in the end. Merry days those were, and I often feel tempted to go and look for the old inn again, but the fear of that piano restrains me. I doubt whether my ear would stand it, now that I know more about pianos. Have you ever eaten cockles ? I always had a basin full, as one of my breakfast dishes, all steaming hot, and thought them excellent. Some time afterwards, when I was in Brittany, they gave me them raw, and expected me to eat them. I forced one open, and a thing like a yellow snail poked out a horn, to find out what the rude man wanted, and when I brandished a knife in my terror, obviously squealed and said, " Please don't." I tried hard to summon up courage, as my hostess evidently thought she had given me a dainty, but my feelings were too much for me, and I resigned the contest. But I do like them boiled. It was a funny coast for shooting. The tide went out an enormous distance, and left a vast mud-flat—good clay mud on which you could safely walk. This was intersected by dykes, where you came on a duck now and then. The whole stretch of mud swarmed with little waders, and there were a fair lot of golden plover. I always shot half-a-dozen of the waders for eating purposes, if I could not get at the plover, and as these latter were as wild as usual, the waders had to suffer, but they were there in their thousands. One man got a pink-footed goose, but I only got a few duck, mostly in the evening; it was so hideously cold sitting out in these muddy dykes, that I wasn't very keen on it. I

wonder if you know the best kind of sight for shooting in the dusk. My old fisherman there taught me. You buy a bit of leather, and press the muzzle of your gun on to it, so as to leave the mark of the barrels, and then cut out the sort of thing that Mr. Williams has drawn for me, and slip it over the muzzle of the gun, and it makes a very effective coarse sight. If you glimpse a duck between those two horns, you'll generally get him. The sand-hills themselves were public, and I got one woodcock, one hare, and a brace of partridges in them, also a short-eared owl, which I shot in ignorance, and which still adorns my room. Poor beast! I was very sorry when I found what I had done. At least I am now; but I'm not very sure that I was then.

Talking of those raw cockles made me think of my little bathing trip to Brittany, which I think you would have enjoyed. There was not much to do except swimming, unless you went out on one of the tunny boats, pretty fishing smacks with a huge rod standing out on each side. It's like trolling for pike: they put on a spinning bait, and when the tunny lays hold, they wind him in with a sort of windlass. It doesn't sound great sport, but they are fine big fish, and the boats look surpassingly pretty on the blue water. We swam, off and on, all day, putting on our bathing costumes directly after breakfast, and going down with a novel to our own special cove. The whole bay was hollowed out into little coves, which we severally appropriated, and no man ever had funnier neighbours on each side than we had. On our left was a little Hungarian and his wife. She used to pretend to be frightened, and run inland: he ran after her, put her over his shoulder, and dived off a rock, with her still over his shoulder. It must have been uncomfortable for her, but as it happened every day, I can only suppose that she liked it. Once in the water, she swam better then he did, and ducked him mercilessly. The French family on the other side were a great contrast. They were papa, mamma, two married sons or daughters, various smaller children, and two nurses. They all lay in a row on their faces, close to one another, just where the waves broke, and kicked their heels, and squealed as the waves broke over them. They never went any farther in, though the water was only four feet deep for about a mile. I suppose they were afraid of the crabs and things which you could see walking about on the bottom, or else they wanted everyone to admire their beautiful bathing costumes. But they *did* amuse us. When we had had a good swim, we sat on a rock, and read our novels, until we wanted to go in again. I got nearly as well pickled as I did in Lincolnshire. The only other thing to do, when you were tired of swimming, was to go inland and eat blackberries, and then chase the great green lizards, some of them quite a foot long, and their tails came off in your hands, and kicked and wriggled. What a funny thing it is that a creature can casually smash off about half of itself, and then go on living, none the worse! I caught one that had half-grown a new tail. I never saw such blackberries. The priests won't let the children pick them, because they say that the crown of thorns was made of brambles, and I found the same superstition in Ireland. I believe I could have gathered a bucketful off a yard of hedge. The whole place was black with them. I very nearly made myself ill, greedy pig! Besides raw cockles, they gave me a slice of ham, sandwiched between two slices of melon, and I liked that very much, though it sounds funny to you, I dare say.

One meets some extraordinarily simple-hearted folk among the sea-going men, small fishermen I suppose, who go out with you on casual duck-shooting expeditions and the like. I recall one bearded giant, who was telling me about a brother of his who had been missing for twenty years. The night before the boat sailed, the widow mother and her two sons had a banquet. She had made two plum-puddings, one to eat, and one to keep till the day when the brother should return. " So he went away and I gave him a kiss on each cheek," said my giant boatman; " I always kissed him, and should do it still, if he came back home again." But there wasn't any home to come to, for the poor old lady, after waiting "nigh on fifteen years," could not wait any longer, and went to look for her lost son, where she probably found him. For when a man is away for fifteen years, instead of two, he doesn't often come back. " And there was still the pudding left, and we put it with her in the coffin, for we thought she'd like to have it when she met him." I was much touched by the pretty story, and the simple matter-of-fact way in which it was told. But that charming simplicity does not prevent them being very keen sportsmen My man always had me out at five or soon after, and the worse the weather, the more he insisted on my turning out, because it would bring the birds in. I shall never forget one specially disgusting morning, when it was blowing hard, and cold showers came hissing at intervals across the water. We had the greatest difficulty in getting over to the island, and as I lay there on the pebble ridges, I almost wished I hadn't been born, especially when I clean missed my first three ducks. However they kept coming, and I managed after a time to hold a bit straighter, and my spirits rose. I had to strike at last against my man's enthusiasm. We had always on previous days gone back to breakfast at nine, with huge appetites, but on this memorable day, nine came and went, and there was no sign of Tom from the far side of the island, only an occasional shot. Ten arrived and I was one duck richer, but my constitution was rapidly breaking up, and I took matters into my own hands and went to fetch Tom, as he showed no signs of coming to fetch me. He was very cross, and pointed to two distant specks, saying plaintively, ''I'd have had one of those for sure." I got him away grumbling lustily, and he growled all the way home about folks not being able to go without breakfast for a bit, and what would I do if I hadn't any breakfast to get, and other conundrums of that sort. I was much

too far gone to dream of trying to guess the answer.
And at half-past eleven, the man was back again, and
took me miles away on that raging ocean, to chase the
wearied duck in queer bays and creeks among the mud-
flats.   I asked him if his wife and family did not want
him for the rest of the day, but he grunted something
about " washing day."   I saw that it was going to be
a washing day for me, as the showers still came sweeping
over, but I had to give in, and really enjoyed my day,
thanks partly to a big packet of sandwiches, and a good
flask of " cold stopper."   But why that boat didn't go
to the bottom I can't say.   She had every chance,
I thought, but I fancy Tom must have handled her with
some skill.   We ought to have got a biggish bag, as
there were lots of duck, and the wind kept them down,
but it was my first try at shooting out of a boat on the
sea, and I found it amazingly difficult to put the shot
anywhere near the object aimed at.   I don't think my
shooting pleased Tom very much, but I pacified him
from time to time, after any especially bad miss, with a
wee drop of mountain dew : and when we came right
on the top of a brace of teal in a mud-gully, and they
both came down to one barrel by a lucky fluke, he looked
upon me with almost a mild and forgiving eye.   What
surprised me most was the power of eyesight in the man.
He could see duck a good twenty seconds before they
came within range of my vision.   I had always rather
fancied my eyesight, but he made an open mockery of
it.   " What duck are those on the water out there ? "
he'd casually observe.

I could see nothing but water anywhere.   I daren't
say " Where ? "   He'd have put me overboard, I firmly
believe.   So I had to sweep the horizon with a wandering
eye, and make a shot.

" Widgeon," says I.

" Widgeon ain't half white," he grunted.

" Oh! which were you looking at ? " seemed to me the only possible answer to save my credit.

" Those three just beyond that streak in the water."

Now the whole ocean was a seething wilderness of choppy waves, and to talk to me of a streak in the water seemed ridiculous, and I said so, and got a pretty dressing down, and was shown the streak, which was certainly there, and three tiny specks beyond it. But as for seeing any white on them, I plainly couldn't. I honestly believe he could, for he was never wrong. The awkward part was, when he turned to me and said, " Now, where's those widgeon of yours ? we'll get to them easier nor the sheldrakes." I thought the farce had gone on long enough, and explained my position, and produced the whisky flask. And after peace was restored, and sarcasm had flowed over me enough, he condescended to give me a lesson in water-craft and eyesight, and I really improved a good five seconds before he had done with me. I never could quite make out whether duck were flying towards or away from me, and it amused him mightily to see me crouch behind the gunwale, and prepare to shoot duck, that were going straight away in the opposite direction. Only once do I remember to have bobbed down before seeing *him* duck his head. It was most humiliating *always* to have to hear " Look out, sir ! " and then after a pause, as I was peering out on the right, " On your left, sir, close to you now." And after I had had many lessons, he took to ducking his head for nothing, just to try me, and after a second or two, leered round and asked me whether it wasn't time to be shooting. I never was so teased and lectured in my life before, but it did me a lot of good, and on subsequent occasions other guardians of my person on salt water have come within measurable distance, not of complimenting me on my eyesight, but of practically saying that I wasn't quite such a fool as I looked. The only other class of persons who come anywhere near a boatman for sheer lack of compliments, and blunt truthfulness in recognising my demerits, are Scotch caddies on the various golf-links which I have mutilated at one time or another, and even they are a long way behind. But perhaps my golf is a trifle better than my shooting.

We didn't get back that day till after five o'clock, and even then Tom had a half desire to stay out on that beastly island again for the evening flight, and it was only the immediate prospect of a parting glass, and a cigar of a particularly vicious brand (the only ones that he allowed to have any taste in them), that got him in, so I cannot say that he did not give me my full money's worth, but I should advise you to think twice before you engage a man to take you duck-shooting on the coast. You'll have to take the rough with the smooth, and be jolly thankful if you get any smooth at all.

I must now confess to a dark deed.

Pray listen, and get over the shock before I go on to describe the scene. I shot a seal. I knew as well as the Ancient Mariner that I had no business to do it, and yet I went and did the deed. I made out three or four good excuses first, for my own satisfaction. One, I wanted the skin for a rug. Two, my boatmen wanted the oil from the blubber to sell to the farmers, who gave a shilling a bottle, because they wanted it to cure their sheep of some disease. So I profited my man, who got twenty bottles, and I hope I cured many sheep. Three, the seals kill the fish, and fish are to feed man primarily. Four, people called me a pig before I did it, so I had to go. I'm sure you ought to be able to pick out of all that lot one good enough to dispose you to listen to the tale I have to tell. Two and four are the ones I fancied most, but please yourself.

I took for the day's outing an Eton boy to back me up in my wickedness, which I thought was a sound move, besides lending an air of respectability to the proceedings. Of course I would have preferred a Winchester man, but I had sent away, two days before, the only specimen I had about me. Besides him, I had two boatmen to row the boat, and my gillie to look after me, and the Eton boy's gillie to look after him. So we were as fine and cheerful a party as ever set sail on the briny deep. For weapons I had my twelve-bore and six cartridges which I had loaded with small bullets, after extracting the ordinary shot. They held nine apiece. Also a sharpened boat-hook to use as a gaff, and two fishing-lines, and some ordinary pike spoons, and a few plain cartridges, in case of duck turning up. We had a five-mile drive first of all, two hundred feet above the sea, which was not the least pleasant part of the day's proceedings. How fish live in that water I don't know, for the cormorants were in flocks of fifty, all busy fishing, and the solan geese were hard at work too, in such numbers that, as they dived and splashed up the water, it looked as if some invisible fleet was bombarding the beautiful expanse of blue, streaked with green and purple shadows. We arrived at our little cove in due time, where we found our boat waiting, with two extraordinary old salts chewing tobacco, and looking as if nothing would ever excite them. They were obviously sceptical about my chances of getting a seal with that gun, but admired the boat-hook. At any rate they started off in a leisurely way, as if they were prepared for an easy and pleasant day, with no great excitement in it. We had to go another five miles across a great bay, dotted with islands, before we were likely to see a seal, but they told me not to shoot, as sound carries a long way over water, so I put away the gun, and of course two duck flew right over our boat directly.

The spoons were trailed out behind, and I got a fine mackerel almost at once. But I may dismiss the fishing briefly by saying that, beyond a few pollack, one of which went off with a spoon and must have been a good one, we got nothing of any account.

At last we began to approach the coast again, just such a coast as seals love. Huge caves into which we could sail with our mast up, and go right in for fully fifty yards, until the opening looked quite a small speck of blue, with a green light dancing on the ceiling from the water, and you hardly dared to speak for fear of breaking the silence; and when a cormorant dived off a high shelf right in front of the boat, it made a sort of whispering echo that fluttered about the roof like a bird's wing. Even if I had seen a seal in any of those caves, I dare not have shot it for fear of the noise, and could not have shot it in such a beautiful and peaceful scene. Outside, all along the coast, were low shelving rocks and tiny rocky islands, which the waves just washed over at about half-tide or lower, and it is on these that the seals bask, while the water just washes their back flippers. It was too high tide when we got there, and the tops of the rocks were not out of the water, so we worked right along the coast, and gazed in wonder at the wild and fantastic rockwork rising high above our heads in pinnacles and spires and buttresses, looking in places just as if giant babies of a Chinese sort of breed had been playing with boxes of bricks, and had littered them about, with bits of queer building done here and there. I should not like to have been among those rocks on anything but a calm day. Even with the little breeze there was, we had to give them a wide berth, as the water was swelling up against them in an ugly kind of way. As we came suddenly round a corner, into a bit of a bay, between us and the rocks there appeared a pair of great eyes on a level with the water, with a bit of head rounded off above them, but it was the eyes that you saw. It was a seal at last, twenty yards off at the outside, and I had my gun up and off in a trice. I thought I was very quick, but he was much quicker, and my bullets only splashed the water where his head had been. The men were a bit excited, and evidently thought I'd done my best. He came up about fifty yards away on the other side, and watched us again with those great weird eyes.

So a council of war was held. It was ultimately decided that I was to scale a small solitary rock covered with little black mussels, while the boat went round and drove him into the bay, so that I'd get a shot at him while he looked at the boat. The idea struck me as quite ingenious, especially as it was my own. I had some bother in getting on to the rock, owing to the nasty swell and the sharp mussels which cut my hands. But I did it, and the boat went off to drive that seal, while I flattened my long person on that very uncomfortable rock. They drove the seal beautifully, only he would watch me all the time and not them. He was a big one, and his head looked extraordinarily like that of a pointer-dog. They all did somehow, in spite of the absence of ears. At last he came up within twenty yards, still watching me. I took a long aim, gazing into those great and solemn eyes, feeling that I was going to commit a murder, and pulled the trigger. But there was no murder in it at all. Even as I pulled the trigger he vanished. I'll swear he watched my finger. He came up again close to me. He didn't wink ; he only looked at me with eyes full of sorrow, to think what wicked intentions filled my heart. And I snapped off cartridge number three viciously and in serious earnest, for I felt that I was being played with. I fancy he must have been only just in time, for he went off in a hurry out to sea, where he remained about fifty yards off and watched us. But I'd had enough of him,

so we ate our lunch, I very sorry for myself, my crew
rather excited and simmering, but still with a sort of
" I told you so " look about them.

Meanwhile my seal had gone, so after lunch we decided
to row a bit farther, and round the very next point, right
in under a vast precipice, blinked another pair of eyes.
Not my old friend, but much the same size ; and I went
for him at once, as he was within easy shot.   I think he
must have caught it just as he turned to dive, for I shot
him clean through the side of the head with two bullets
close together.   You should have heard the howl that
those men raised.   The whole boat was in danger of
being capsized as they rushed for the oars.   We got there
just in time, as he was beginning to sink, and the boat-
hook just got enough hold to pull up his hind flippers,
round which they tied a rope in no time.   He was stone
dead, thank goodness, so I did not mind the way he bled.
I only mention the fact for two reasons.   The first is,
that they all agreed that seals' blood in the water meant
a bad storm, and I just hit off that storm for a thirty-mile
drive two days after, on my way home, with the wind
and rain full in my face.   Bad luck to their superstitions
and prophecies ! and the other reason is, that having
got my seal, I went for another on the way home, and
the fact that there was no blood proved to me, after the
sight of that red ocean at the death of number one, that
I had not hurt him, which was a satisfaction.   We got
the first seal on board after much hauling, for he was
over six feet long, and in fine condition, and started
home, a noisy crew.   But suddenly we heard the seals
singing too.   I never heard the noise before, and it was
most striking amid that wild scene of rocks and waters.
A sort of plaintive lament, like a merman with a cold
in his head.   It quieted my crew down at once, and
they so took it for granted that I'd use my other two
cartridges, that I felt inclined to do so myself.   Nor was

the opportunity wanting. The rocks were out of water now, and we spied a veritable monster, much bigger than my victim, lying on a single rock, with another and higher rock within easy gun-shot. So we did a great and silent stalk, keeping the higher rock between us and our intended prey. I thought we'd never get there, but we did at last, and then I thought I'd never climb that rock : but in the end I did, and peeped over. There was my giant. I smothered my excitement, and fired at the back of his head. He scarcely stirred at the shot, and I jumped up and howled for the boat. They again tumbled over oars and thwarts, in a wild state of excitement. I thought they'd never come, but they did at last, with much splashing and yelling, my gillie waving the boat-hook round his head, and exhorting the rowers with mellow howls. It was just as well that they were too late by about fifteen yards, for if that boat-hook had got well planted, there'd have been either a man overboard (they none of them could swim !), or the whole boat upset ; most likely the latter, for they would have all rushed yelling to the side to lend a hand. But as I say, they were too late. I saw to my horror the head slowly uplifted, and then, quicker than I can write it, he slipped back into the water, and was gone with a whisk of his tail. I snapped my last cartridge recklessly at the boil in the water, but thank goodness there was no spot of blood on the rock, or anywhere else. The bullets must have glanced off his hard skull, and only stunned him. One of the men muttered that he hadn't liked only hearing one shot at first, and of course I could easily have given him another barrel as he lay there, but I was so sure that he was stone dead, that I never thought of it, and now I am glad only to have one seal down to my score, but he *was* a whacker, and at the time I called all the gods to witness my grief and sorrow. I could not get the men away for a long time ; they tried to rake the bottom of the ocean with that boat-hook ; but there was some whisky left, and by the help of that, and the sight of our one splendid seal, we at last plucked up energy enough to go on our way.   We saw beautiful scenes on the way home.   Five great seals basking on one rock, and nearly fifty more heads working in to the coast in all directions. One veritable grandfather of all the seals popped his head up close to us, and after one solemn look, vanished in a great boil of water.   I was most unwilling to go away from such a scene, but time was pressing, and the wind was beginning to rise, thanks to that seal's blood in the water, and so we tore ourselves away.   I had one more bit of luck on the way home, getting two big brown ducks.   I can't even now make out what they were. They were quite big, and their plumage rather reminded me of a grouse, very dark with golden-brown tips to the feathers.   Someone called them young eiders.   They were quite good to eat anyway.   Not a bit fishy, and beautifully tender, and I should have liked some more. But on the whole I was very well content with my day, and the skin makes a very fine rug, to remind me of all that gorgeous coast.

I've never done much cliff-climbing by the sea, nor should I feel justified, even if I had, in advising you to try it, as it is dangerous work, however cool your head may be, and however sure your foot.   Still I have very little doubt, had I had cliffs handy, instead of the flat lands of Lincolnshire, when I was your age, that I should have made my way about them somehow, as I dare say some of you do.   But I did have one very jolly day down behind the Needles in the days when eggs were not so carefully guarded as they are now.   I can't call it cliff-climbing, but it was a pleasant scramble, with just enough chance of hurting myself rather badly to make it exciting. I got a boat and man at Alum Bay, and after a look over the Needles Lighthouse, which was the first I had ever inspected (I saw some fine convolvulus hawk moths pinned on the wall, which had flown against the glass), we went round under some of the highest white cliffs in the world, I suppose, where the cries of the sea-birds nearly deafened me, and the razorbills (rosabells, my man called them) and guillemots and puffins came buzzing like cannon-balls over .the boat, while the gulls hung poised overhead in a white cloud, and told us very plainly what they thought of us. We found a place to land, with difficulty, and then scrambled up tiny precipices crowned with grassy slopes—a summer sea crowned with bowery hollows—till we were high enough up to make me quite certain that I was going no farther. But I sat there for half-an-hour, in spite of the almost savage protests of the gulls, and thought how jolly it was, and how singularly unpleasant that downward journey would be, and how I wished I was safe back in my little boat.

I got safe back without any adventures, but with a pleasant tingling in my blood and finger-tips, the richer by two or three lots of herring-gull's eggs, which I had taken from their nests of grass and rubbish on the rocks, as I came down : also one pair of cormorant's eggs, out of a smelly nest of sea-weed at rather a nasty corner, and one puffin's out of a hole in the rock. So that I got some reward for my fright and excitement, and was very popular for a while with a few of my boy friends, who had an eye to the superfluous eggs of the herring-gull and got them too. It was a very small expedition, but enough to show me what the charms of rock-climbing are, and how they can lay hold of a man till they lead him to his end. And I had the same feeling once again in Ireland, when my wife and an old shepherd took me a walk along the cliffs of Slieve League in Donegal, and we suddenly came upon a nice little piece of pathway, about twenty yards long, with a rough step a yard high in the middle of it, and a drop of two thousand feet on

one side and four hundred on the other. On the two-
thousand side I made out that I should have touched
once pretty heavily before I reached the sea ; on the
other I should have bumped a good deal, but the result
would have been much the same. I took it sitting down
with one leg over each side, paying very strict attention
to the ground directly in front of me, and thinking of
other engaging things like " ham and eggs," " cold
plum-pudding," anything in fact to divert my mind from
the view on each side, which would keep whispering
" Look at me." " Not I," I replied ; " just wait till
I'm across this bit of switchback."

When I did reach " terra-firma " beyond, I inspected
that terrible pathway from a very safe place, where I
had none of the desire to chuck myself over and have
done with it, which had been somewhere at the back of
my mind during my anxious transit, and registered a
vow that that should be the last time I would inspect
my old friend the sea from such a very uncanny altitude.
That vow I have kept, and my more recent acquaintance
with it has been confined to pottering about rocky pools,
where the mermaids wash their hair at night, leaving a
few long trails of it to show that they have been there,
and the sea-anemones open their red and feathery hearts
and clasp their prey. And if you ask my advice I say,
" Cultivate the sea at close quarters, and don't try to put
yourself at any foolish elevation above an old friend,
lest your pride have a fall."

CHAPTER VIII

RATTING, RABBITING, AND THE LIKE

It is always a matter of wonder to me how every boy, myself included, combines within himself an intense desire to kill and an equally intense desire to pet and make friends with animals and living creatures generally. Show a boy a lot of birds, on a day dumb and dead with snow and frost, scrambling for crumbs on a patch which has been swept green for them, and obviously so starved that they have forgotten to be wary, and the odds are anything you like that he says : " Where's my catapult ? "

But give him the same birds in an aviary, and he is never quite happy until he has made them so tame that they all mob him, sitting on his shoulders and head, and all over him, whenever he comes to feed them. And the same holds equally good with rats, and rabbits, and badgers, and weasels, and such small deer. He will keep a tame rat in his pocket, and squeal with delight if he can make it eat out of the same plate with him ; but put it in the open, and give him a stick and there is very little chance that the rat will ever enter his pocket except as a corpse.   He will brave the surliest of gardeners, and trample down a whole carrot bed to feed his tame rabbits ; but give him a gun, a ferret, and a net, or a wire, and he will denude the country of rabbits if he possibly can, and he generally can.   I often wonder that Australia, when overwhelmed by rabbits, did not import boys instead of weasels : she would have done the business more thoroughly, and have found it cheaper in the end, I think.   I have no doubt it is a curious relic of our animal nature.   My dogs have it.   My Irish terrier Mike loves his own cat in the house, and licks her all over till she is a wet mop of wool, but if he catches her in the open he will kill her.   He let my squirrel bury nuts in his coat, but he caught that squirrel abroad one day, and there was a cage to let at once.   And not only that, but when fond hands buried him, he dug him up and scattered him abroad, so that they no more said, " Here lies Sammy."

I don't quite know which a boy loves best, rats or sparrows.   I say " loves " advisedly.   We boys show our loves in queer ways, and our love of these two cheap creatures mostly takes the form of persecuting them. But however much we persecute them—and I for one have persecuted them beyond measure—I am quite certain that I should find it hard to name a bird and a beast that are dearer to my heart.   I suppose it is really the memory of many happy days—happy to us at any rate, if not to them—that so consecrates them in our affections, the little brown bird and the little brown beast. I doubt whether they love us quite so much, but I am not at all sure.   I cannot name any other bird or beast among the wild animals that dogs our footsteps so closely. Wherever man goes, there goes the sparrow and there goes the rat.   I can almost imagine one of them writing somewhat in this same way about us.   For really, when you come to think of it, the damage is not all on our side. It is quite a possible view for a sparrow or a rat to take, that we are poor persecuted creatures, that they do love us dearly, but that they can't think we have any great affection for them, so perhaps we are both right to love the other.

However, to settle which is more necessary to a boy's happiness is about as difficult as to offer a man his choice between a day's shooting and a day's fishing. And I dare say we shall have room in this chapter to talk a little between ourselves, of the charms that lurk in the pursuit of both of these darlings of ours, without laying ourselves open to the charge of being utterly inhuman monsters.

Many are the ways of pursuing the sparrow. One does not talk of pursuing other birds much, though they get killed accidentally now and then, and on the whole we are sorry when they do. But the sparrow we definitely pursue, with intent to kill him in cold blood. I don't think any decent boy ought to try to kill a chaffinch, any more than he would a robin or a wren : but there is a sort of licence granted, even by the tenderest hearted of maiden aunts, to kill sparrows. And here again it is very hard to say which of all the primitive ways of capture and destruction, putting guns out of the question, is the more full of joyous memories. Whether it be the well-constructed and deadly brick trap, or the nimble but erratic garden riddle, or the catapult liable to confiscation, or the net by night on the ivied wall, or when one is tired of these better known and more certain methods of capture, some of the many other ways which I hope that boys can still invent, which may get their one or two victims, or may fail. It is a proud moment when you catch a sparrow for the first time in some trap, or by some device, of your own construction. For after all it is a very fair battle between boy and sparrow, as far as skill

goes, though the sparrow has more at stake, namely his
neck, as a rule—but goodness knows! I risked mine often
enough. How I have watched that riddle, with fingers
trembling on the cord, while robins, and tits, and finches,
and even jackdaws, stole the dainties, while the wily
sparrows sat in a compact circle about a yard outside
the radius of danger—the fire-zone, so to speak—and
were content to gather up the crumbs spilt by their more
privileged brethren. It was never till hope was almost
exhausted, that one would venture under that suspicious
object, even though the well-fed robin sat on the top,
and told them to "buck up" and then he just grabbed
a bit and bolted. Did you ever catch more than two
sparrows at a time under a riddle ? I don't think I ever
did.

The brick-trap of course is more deadly, except that
the robin *will* get in first, and sometimes gets caught by
the head and killed. Which same disaster comes home
to my remembrance very strongly, for my mother always
made me close my traps for a day when it happened,
and I never remember to have neglected her wish, even
though I could easily have buried the corpse and said
nothing about it. It only shows how loyal boys are in
some matters.

The other curious fact is, that it came to be a sort of
accepted treaty between Billy and me, that if we could
catch the dead robin artistically in the other fellow's trap,
without being detected either in the act or by a post-
mortem, which would reveal a sort of double fracture
(we knew pretty accurately how much a falling brick
crushed a robin's skull), the other fellow closed *his* trap
—the penalty for detection being two days trapless.
It was a great risk to run, because we knew each other's
movements pretty well, and could lie as low as an
ambushed Indian.

I well remember how Billy did me once. His trap killed a robin, and he got the corpse artistically deposited in mine, and then climbed a fir tree near his own, and watched me come and take the carcass, and plant it in his trap, whereupon he hailed me with shouts of derision.

Our life was never dull in those happy days, and we grew up rather wide-awake in most matters. But I got level with him later on rather unexpectedly. I was watching some sparrows round my trap, close to hedge, out of a hiding-place of my own, when they suddenly bolted, and to my amazement I saw an arm come through

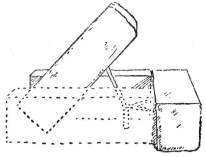

the hedge, and let the brick of my trap down with great care. I was almost too startled to yell, but I got it out of my mouth in time, and the dead robin was there all right, and so was Billy, and so I shut his trap for two days, and neither of them was a Sunday, and I was as pleased as if I had got that sparrow for which I had been waiting, and rather better pleased. A boy's instinct as to what is real cheating and what is honest is eccentric, but I think based on sound sense. The mother said a trap was to be closed, and we obeyed rigidly, as I hope you do; but we planted frauds on one another.

I have just discovered two boys, otherwise worthy of the name, who have never heard of a brick-trap. I rather hope I have bagged the only two ignoramuses (or ignorami), but as there seems room for doubt, I believe I must tell you briefly the points of a brick-trap. You want four well-made bricks, a level bit of ground, and three pieces of stick. Put two bricks side by side, with a third standing on end between them, so as to get them the right distance apart. The upright brick ought just not to touch the brick on each side ; then put the other one across the end of the two, so as to touch both. It is not a bad thing to hammer down a wooden peg outside this one, to keep it tight in its place, as the upright one has to fall on it, and may knock it down, if you don't secure it. Now for the sticks. Number one is about four or five inches long, about half as thick as a good walking-stick. This you sharpen at one end, and cut off quite level at the other, then push it into the ground, so that *not more* than two inches are left above ground, right in the middle of the three bricks which are lying on their narrower sides. Next you cut a stick with a fork, like a small merry-thought, and shave off the thick end on both sides, till it comes nearly to have an edge —this edge goes on to the top of the stick in the ground, with the merry-thought, or two points, pointing towards the end brick. Lastly comes a piece of stick, a trifle thinner than the one in the ground, about three inches long, one end of which holds the forked stick, between itself and the first piece, and the other end supports the brick which was upright, but which is now tilted forward, so that if you knock the sticks down, it just falls nicely on to the front brick.

Then sprinkle plenty of crumbs inside, and a few on the edge and round the trap. When a bird wants the crumbs inside the bricks, he jumps on to the forked stick, which falls down and pulls away the bit of stick which holds up the brick. If you set the trap clumsily, so that the brick does not fall clean and quick, the bird has just time to pop its head out again, and so gets killed. But you ought to try once or twice with a stone, to make sure that everything works well, as it is horrid to find a dead robin. To get the bird out, you either lift the top brick enough to get your hand in, or slide one of the side bricks back a bit, but I should peep first, as I once got a small rat, and as I put my hand straight in without first looking, he got me too and I bled pretty freely. It is delicious to peep round a corner and find your trap with the brick down, and almost more delicious to hide, and watch the sparrows squabbling round it. You think they are never going in, when suddenly down it goes, and you know that there is one roast sparrow for tea at any rate.

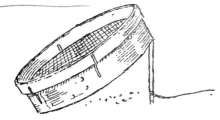

The riddle wants no explanation—you prop it up with a stick, tie a long string to the stick, and when the birds go under for the crumbs, pull the stick away. The difficulty is to get them out, as they dodge about, and, if you leave the smallest possible opening, out they go. You sometimes get aggravated, just as the birds are coming nicely, by an old hen or duck marching up and upsetting the whole thing.

Now for the nicest thing of all, and that is stack and ivy hunting at night with a lantern, and a net or riddle tied on to two poles or one, according to which you use, or even with your own hands and nothing else. It does perhaps seem rather hard lines to hunt them, after they have gone to bed, but I never could resist it, it was too fascinating. Apart from the mere catching of birds, the whole surroundings are so delicious, especially if you do as I did, and go alone for choice. This means that you can't use a net, as it requires two poles and so two men. But I never quite liked a net, partly, as I say, because you couldn't go alone, and partly because it is rather butchery. For, if there are enough sparrows, you may easily catch thirty or forty in an evening. Still if you want to do it, the method is simple. You either make or buy a good big square of net, and tie it on to two good poles, and go out after dark, and clap it on to the ivy, and pull it down, and take the sparrows out. Nothing could be simpler. But I never cared for big bags, if they were made too easily, and with no skill. What I did enjoy was principally the feeling of being alone in the dark, I believe. As a child I hated and dreaded it, but this dread grew up into a sort of delicious feeling of running all sorts of risks, which made me feel nice and creepy at all the corners, just as if something was coming round the opposite way, which would nab me, if I didn't look out.

I did actually walk into a cow once, and I really cannot express my feelings. I don't think I ever knew before what being in a blue and deadly funk meant. If anyone had been with me, we should have only laughed. But as it was, I was simply too frightened to squeal. I might just have been turned to stone. It really was rather delicious. If you have never been out in the dark quite alone, just go out and try what it feels like. You'll come home extraordinarily quickly the first night, and for a night or two after that. I'll almost defy you not to. The mice are rustling about ; the wind sounds eerie and dangerous in the trees ; if there is a moon with clouds, the whole night is full of ghosts rushing about ; every bush is a goblin or something worse, and the more you look at them, the more they either seem to be moving stealthily towards you, or to be crouching for a spring.

And I almost think that the worst nights of all are those when nothing is happening, absolutely nothing, no mice, no wind, no shadows, only a huge and monstrous expectation of something just going to happen. We go out bravely, ready for adventures, and nothing happens, and then we gradually realise that we are utterly and absolutely and helplessly alone in the world, but that it won't last long. The very silence makes our ears sing, and we go slower and slower, just as if we were gradually turning to stone. It is boojum hunting : we are going to vanish away softly and silently, oh ! so silently. It's a delicious feeling, when you get a bit used to it, and whenever I feel at all tired or worried, I go out even now, and try to feel creepy. But before you get used to it, it's just awful. You can't run home, because you know that, directly you turn your back, you're grabbed for certain by something worse than any ordinary monster so you have to sidle home half backwards, unless you can eventually pluck up courage to go on.

But enough of these terrors, fascinating though they are. You never quite get over them : there is always enough left to give interest to the proceedings. Sometimes I went off with my lantern only, and poked my hand into the holes in the thatch of the sheds, getting here and there a sparrow, and sometimes a wren or tit, which latter always bit me hard, and was let go quietly, so as to frighten the brave little man as little as possible, and once or twice even a small rat or a big mouse—I never quite made out which, for they always bit badly— and then when I pulled out my hand to suck it, fled into

M

the darkness.   I always vowed I'd hold and slay the next
one, but never could manage to keep hold after getting
bitten.   More often I tied the garden riddle on to a short
pole and worked along the stacks, just where the thatch
comes down, or spotted likely places in the ivy.   The
great secret of success was to watch where they roosted,
and mark it carefully in one's mind : for things look so
different by lamplight.   Often when I was sure that I
had the right place exactly, and dabbed the riddle on,
there was a scurry of wings, and a lot of little agitated
half-seen figures scrambling off post-haste into the
darkness, which seemed to hang round like a thick curtain.
They got the trick of sleeping with one eye open after
a while, and directly I held up the light to see where to
plant the riddle, off went two or three cunning old cocks.
I nearly always had one companion in my nocturnal
wanderings, and that was our old black cat, who had
hopes of a bird for herself, and generally got one, after
I had reasonably provided for the morrow's tea.   I liked
to have her company.   I thought she'd keep off the
worst witches, with whom she was probably in league.
Besides these things, I sometimes took my butterfly net,
and went very quietly into a shed, and stood the lantern
so as to shine on a patch of wall, and then knocked the
rafters.   The birds generally fly first to the patch of
light, but you have to be very quick with the net, as
they soon realise their mistake, and make off on the line
where they smell the fresh air, and vanish into the dark.
    Those are the ways to catch sparrows.   Blackbirds I
went for sometimes, to save next year's strawberries.
But I never much liked to kill the jolly old gentlemen,
and soon gave it up.   They roost in the hedgerows, and
you send someone with a lantern on one side (a sister
will do, if she has generally been behaving well, and
deserves a treat), to shine it into the hedge : you walk

on the dark side yourself with a rather long and rather strong stick, and when you see the blackbird crouching in the hedge, and staring at the light, which you will do very plainly if the lantern is well held, you use your stick like a lance, and smite him with one end of it. But you have to make a very straight shot, and don't push it far through the hedge, or you may get your sister, and then there'll probably be a row, as girls don't always understand that sort of thing. On the whole, unless the blackbirds are too numerous, and want killing down, I don't advise you to hunt the hedges a great deal, though it is pretty and skilful work in its way.

I come now to a more dangerous and risky form of sport—that is, catapults and other such engines. Dangerous they are both to you and to others. To you, because they may easily get you into trouble ; and to others, because you may quite possibly put someone's eye out. I never did do it actually, but I was near enough once or twice to give me a great warning how careful one ought to be ; nor did I ever get into any personal inconvenience from the use of them myself, but inasmuch as, in my later years, I have been responsible for other boys sitting uneasily (what a shame, isn't it ?) I know that such inconvenience is quite within the bounds of possibility, and think it only fair to warn you.

The catapult, as ordinarily made by a boy, is a clumsy and unskilful weapon, and worse than that, very hard to conceal in an emergency. But perhaps you ought to begin with a pretty big one, and then learn more dainty weapons. Seek the hedgerows then till you find a stick with a pretty fork, as narrow as possible. Hawthorn is a very good wood. Then strip off the bark, and boil it to make it tough. Take two lengths of round catapult elastic, not too thick, about a foot long. The difficulty is to fasten these neatly to the two forks, so that the

wood does not chafe them.   They will break there any
way sooner or later, but a little care will make them
last much longer.   I used to put a bit of old glove
between the elastic and the stick, and when I had nearly
done the splice, another bit between the fine string and
the elastic.   But it is difficult to do it all neatly.   At the
other end it is easy to splice on a little flap of old glove,

as a pouch for the shot or small
stone.   I have no doubt that with
a little practice you will make as
neat a weapon as ever I could
produce, and I could generally
sell mine for half - a - crown at
school.

Personally, I did not use these
clumsy ones for long.   I soon
adopted two pieces of penholder,
each shaved off at one end, so that
you could lash them together into
a tiny fork, with a single strand
on each side of the thin square
elastic one buys in balls, and a
tiny pouch, and a single shot of
about number four size, and later
on still I chucked the penholder,
and fastened the two strands of
elastic on to my thumb and fore-
finger with just a simple loop.   This is an extraordinarily
invisible weapon ; the mere closing of your hand is quite
enough to hide it, let alone putting your hand into your
breeches pocket.   I doubt whether many boys realise
what a deadly weapon this is, up to pretty nearly twenty
yards.   It is so silent, that you will get two or three
chances at the same bird, unless you happen to hit a twig
close to him.

I have seen a sparrow, when the shot went just past him, shake himself, and ruffle out his feathers, as if something quite innocent had just touched him. It is amazing how accurate you may get with this little bit of elastic on your fingers, and one small shot. I had a friend at school for whom I would willingly hold up a penny between my fingers at ten yards, and never knew him touch my fingers once. He used to flick the buttons off the back of our Sunday tail-coats, if we walked past his windows on our way to chapel, and in the dormitories we threw up our soap, and he would put a shot through it, three out of five times, even by gaslight. I expect you think that I am putting it on a bit, but I assure you I am not : and if this by any accident should meet his eye, he'll tell you the same tale. You may judge for yourself, whether sparrows flourished in the neighbourhood of our school. Thanks to my cooking skill, they were all utilised, as we had studies with fire-places in them. I don't say that you can ever shoot as straight as this, for he was well above the average, but I could always make a bigger bag with this little toy weapon than with the clumsier stick catapult, and the chances of being detected were almost nothing. Perhaps that is why I think that boys nowadays don't know so much as I did. They may know it all, and keep it away from my magisterial eyes. All I beg of you, if I have taught you too much, is that you should never shoot without looking to see if a human eye is anywhere near, as one shot can kill an eye as well as a sparrow.

In Lincolnshire I used a bow and arrow : the bow being a briar cut out of the hedge, strung with an ordinary piece of good string, and the arrow a reed out of the dykes, with a nail filed as sharp as a needle lashed into one end, the other end being cut off at a knot, so that the bowstring would not split it. And strange to say I killed a bird now and then, but not very often, even with this primitive weapon, as also with a stone jammed into a split stick, and even a sling made of two bootlaces and a piece of strong leather. It is very difficult to keep straight with this latter. David must have been pretty good to get Goliath first shot. You fasten one lace tight round your forefinger, and whirl it round and round your head, and then let go the other lace, which you have been holding loosely. You had better go a long way from windows and people to practise, but after a time you will find that you can generally put a stone there or thereabouts, and as it goes a longish way, you can reckon on dumping a stone down well in the middle of a flock of sparrows feeding, and getting one sometimes, and every sparrow got in a new way is something to be proud of. Of course you must learn to throw a stone straight with your hand. I certainly had one period in my eventful career, when I could reckon on hitting the bird, if the bird did not fly away before the stone got there. At any rate I kept a pair of young owls for nearly a month solely on birds got by throwing stones at them, and they weren't starved either. I grant that some days I had Billy throwing on the other side of the hedges, which makes a lot of difference, as the blackbird, honest gentleman, doesn't quite know which side to come out,

and so you get an easy shot or two. But it is very easy
to learn to throw extraordinarily straight : and it is a
gift which lasts a long time, until your muscles get stiff.
I certainly killed birds by throwing, up to the age of
thirty. There's a confession for a schoolmaster !

Now I must really drop my beloved sparrows, much
against my will, or I shall have no room for the nimble
rat, and he is a dear good friend, whom I can confidently
advise you to become acquainted with, if you do not
know him and love him already. The beauty of him is,
that everyone blesses you for killing him : and yet I
don't know : he's a brave sportsman, and I always felt
inclined to fire a salute over his corpse.

I hate those nasty traps with teeth, but one has to use
them sometimes. Let us cut them very short. The one
consolation is, that the rat will generally beat you, and
I feel rather a beast to tell you the certain way to get
him, and that is, cover up the trap with leaves, or straw,
or what you will, but don't put the bait on the trap.
Let it dangle in the air, with a stick and thread, just so
high directly above the trap, that a rat can reach it and
no more. He is almost certain either to forget the trap,
or overbalance into it, in his efforts to get the bait. And
look at your trap just before you go to bed, so as to kill
him, if possible, almost directly he gets caught. So
much for what is sometimes a necessity.

Now for rats in a house, and how to get at them. You
can't ferret them very well, and poisons I hate. Besides,
they are dangerous, and a dead rat smells. Well, you
can take a wash-tub, filled half-way up with earth, with
a ladder up the side of some sort ; a rat can climb almost
anything. Give them food in this for two or three
nights. They can jump out easily. And then when they
are used to it, empty out the earth, and fill it carefully
half-full of water, and sprinkle the surface of the water

thickly with bran, about an inch and a half, or the water
will soak through.   Mr. Rat thinks it all right, and jumps
on to the bran and gets drowned.   It is ingenious, but
not much sport, only interesting.   A better game is, to
take a small cellar with only one door and no windows,
but the kitchen will do, and is almost better fun.   Scatter
a bit of food in that room every night, and see that it
is very hard to find any anywhere else, so that every rat
in the house will get well used to going to that room
for his dinner or supper, and then one night tie a long
string to the door, so that you can pull it to with certainty
from a long way off.   Practise a bit in the daytime, if
the cook will let you, and she will, if you have properly
digested my first chapter, for it does not do to make
any mistake.   Let the house be quite quiet for about an
hour after everyone has gone to bed, and then pull hard
at the string and call your pals.   Do you remember that
chapter in " Hereward," where he and Martin Lightfoot
put a ladder across the doorway ?   I had a lovely picture
in my copy, with the remark printed underneath, " And
then began a murder grim and great," and I always think
of that picture when I go downstairs after pulling the
string.   Let me advise you, unless you like the feel of
a rat up your leg, to tuck your breeches into your
stockings.   And unless you have a dog with you, one
or two rats are pretty certain to elude you, and hide till
you are gone.   But it is really splendid fun to be in a
kitchen full of rats, with a stick and a candle.   Bad for
the crockery, do you say ?   Well, perhaps !   But the
cook ought to have put it away.   Anyway a house cleared
of rats is worth a pie-dish or two.

But it is not often that one can indulge in these battues :
the ordinary run of sport with rats is by the agency of
ferrets.   As to the management of ferrets, I have already
told you all I know in my chapter on Pets.   We will

take it for granted that you have two or three, and know
how to take proper care of them.

Of course, you can always get a day at rats, without
ferrets, if you keep an eye on the stacks, and go to them
on threshing-day, but there is generally rather a mob of
dogs and men with sticks. Still there is always a certain
amount of fun, including sore shins, to be got out of
mixing in a mob of dogs and men with sticks, all wild
with excitement ; and I have no doubt that you are active
enough to get your share of the sport. I heard an old
farmer say of me on one such occasion, not twenty years
ago, "Dang me if that long-legged parson ain't worth
all the dogs put together," and I thought it rather a nice
compliment. But I wasn't so well pleased when he took
me into the parlour afterwards, and insisted on my
drinking beer, which was not by any manner of means
the nut-brown ale of old England, but a very sorry and
sour decoction of more than doubtful malt and hops.
Greatness has its penalties.

But to come back to our ferrets : anyone will allow
the joys of hunting outlying ricks and banks with these
merry pets, who has ever enjoyed a late October day of
this kind. You may get fun of a larger kind with hounds
or gun, but a good day's ratting is bad to beat. When
you have carefully stopped all the bottom holes round a
lowish corn-stack, and chucked four or five ferrets up
on to the top, and seen them all go to ground keen and
eager, then there comes a moment of really good and
exciting expectation. Suddenly you hear a whack with
a stick on the far side of the stack, then perhaps a cry
of disgust, which means a miss, then a howl of " Mark
over the top," and down comes a lusty great rat full
tilt, probably ending in a flying leap ; and if you take
him nicely in mid-air, with a neat back-hander, and land
him three or four yards away, " dead as a rat," and then

have time to snick another, as he scurries along a pathway they have made just under the eaves of the thatch, you have no cause to complain either of your quickness of sight or readiness of hand.   The only warning I would give you is, look before you hit, and never hit unless you can see.   A short-sighted friend of mine once horrified me by rushing full tilt in great excitement, and smiting a real good ferret full across the back, as he was just sniffing outside the stack to see where the rat had gone, killing him as dead as could be.   And you may very easily do the same, even without being short-sighted. When you have worked the rats well down to the bottom, then unstop the bottom holes, and give the ferrets a turn there.   You'll have to be as quick as lightning here with your stick, as the rat almost as soon as he is out of one hole is into another.   Still there is just time, if you are nimble : and even if you miss now and then, I still maintain that it is difficult to find better sport or better training for eye and hand.   I believe if I had to make a racket-player I'd start him on a month's ratting.   Just now and then you'll get a stack that the ferrets won't face after the first ten minutes.   I well remember one. We put in Jenny and Sally and Brown Bess and the White Rabbit and a couple of young 'uns that had done nothing to earn names.   And one after another they all came out, bitten and bleeding and cowed.   There was a general cry for vengeance, and " Fetch out Maria."   Maria was a big old brown lady, who was generally kept for emergencies.   She was hauled out rather sulky, for she was very idle, and after sundry shakes reconnoitred various holes, and chose one into which she squeezed herself, all but the tip of her tail.   We saw from the tail that she gave a start back and a start forward, and then she slowly backed out, pulling an enormous buck-rat after her, with a big bite just over her own eye.   She was very grumpy and cross, and after giving up her victim with great reluctance, refused to do any more work, so we had to leave the stack, but we got our vengeance some weeks later, when it was threshed out, to the tune of something over a hundred rats, some of them very big. I couldn't have believed it would hold so many : there couldn't have been much corn. No wonder Jenny and her sisters had rather a rough time.

Besides stacks, there are also the hedgerows, which are best in the earlier autumn, say the latter end of September, before the rats have made their way into the stacks. But it is difficult work, as there is such a lot of undergrowth that a fair shot with a stick is almost impossible. Still if you begin at one end, and work the rats on and on to the other, being careful not to let any get back, you will pick up one here and there by a lucky shot, and get them into the open at last. Your best chance is a gateway, with a drain-pipe underneath it. Look well for this before you begin, and stop up the far end carefully. When you get up to it, you may find as many as ten or a dozen rats huddled into it : then you can clear the ground a bit, and one of you will go to the far end and one to the near end, and push them out first to one and then to the other with a couple of long sticks. Then you stop the end that wasn't stopped before, and work the rest of the bank from the far end up to the gateway again, leaving someone to guard the gateway, so that the rats don't get across into the holes which you have already worked, and the tragedy of the drain-pipe is repeated.

A pig-sty or two will finish up your day well : dirty work, but great fun, as the pigs rather enter into it, even to the extent of going for one of the ferrets if they get a chance. They like fresh meat, and will generally eat a young rat. I sometimes gave them one, as a thank-

offering for a merry half-hour. Whether it improved
the flavour of the bacon or not, someone else must say.
One word of advice I may perhaps give ; and that is,
always ask leave of the farmer before you go on to his
ground. He is glad as a rule to have his rats killed,
but he would rather be asked civilly than come and find
you doing it without leave. In the one case you may
find a reward of real fine apples put in your way, and in
the other you may be turned off neck and crop, and lose
a good day and many others. Besides, nobody really
likes the kind of boy who takes it for granted that he
may go anywhere and do anything just as he pleases.
I like a boy with plenty of cheek, but I do like it rather
hidden away for emergencies and special occasions. So
now you know my views.

Now I have just got a bit of dangerous ground for
my finish, so we must go warily. What about rabbits ?
They are varmints that have got many a poor man into
trouble, who had much more need, possibly, of one,
than I hope you will ever feel. Perhaps the best thing
will be, to suppose that one of your friends, the farmers,
has suggested that you should have a day at them in one
of his banks, and then we can talk freely about it, without
fear of the law. Two bits of knowledge are necessary—
how to muzzle ferrets, and how to make and manage a
little rabbit net. For the first : take a bit of thin string
and tie a loop, that won't run, about half-way : this loop
has got to stand up between the ears : don't make it
much bigger than will just let the string pass through :
now bring one end down each side of the neck, and tie
them reasonably tight (but mind you don't throttle him)
with a double knot under his neck : then bring both
ends together, and tie the two together into a knot half-way
under his nose, pass one each side of his nose, and tie
them with a single knot on the top, tight enough to keep

his mouth shut, bring one end through the little loop standing up between his ears, and back down his forehead where it ought to meet the other end. Tie the two ends off with a double knot, which ought to come about the middle of the forehead, and cut the ends off close. That makes what I think the most comfortable muzzle. Some people slip a little nail behind their long teeth, and fasten it with string over the nose, and round the nail on each side of the mouth, and tied off underneath, which is perhaps simpler, but I don't care for it so much as the other.

The nets are not so easy to describe. Net with fairly fine string, and about an inch mesh (if you can't net,

you certainly ought to learn), a net about a yard long and two feet wide. Gather all the loops of one of the narrow ends into a small brass ring. Take a piece of good strong string nearly eight feet long, and run one end, first through the brass ring, and then through every outside loop all the way round the other three sides of the net, and then back through the brass ring, so that you have about a yard clear of the ring at each end. Fasten the two ends tight to a strong peg. Now let us go quietly to our bank. You cannot go too quietly. Look for a small bolt hole, not the main entrance. You'll want about three nets to

cover all possible exits.   Peg the main stick tight into
the ground about a foot above the hole, and spread the
net over the hole loosely ; if it is windy, you had better
put a tiny peg or two down the sides, just tight enough
to keep the net in place and no more.   Keep far the
greater half of the net below the hole.   Now put a ferret
into the main entrance, and keep very still out of sight
of the holes.   The rabbit bolts against the net, which
all runs up into a bag with the rabbit inside, and the
more he kicks the tighter it holds.   And remember to

kill him quick, for his own sake, and to replace the net
quick for yours, as there is most likely another or two.
Only don't stamp about—move as quietly as ever you
can, or they will refuse to bolt.   And don't walk off with
the rabbits at the end, for they belong to the farmer.
He will probably give you a couple.

   And one word more : if you should ever happen to
be—well, we won't call it trespassing, but—looking at
rabbit-holes on doubtful territory, which, being a boy
you may find yourself obliged to do for the sake of your
self-respect, just now and then, and if there should happen

to be a ferret about and a net, as there may be for the same reasons, and if again you should happen to view in the distance a doubtful character, like a master who does not understand such things, coming your way, stuff the net into the hole that the ferret is likely to come out of, and sit on it, and admire the view, and put on that look of angelic innocence, which you can doubtless assume in your wickedest moments, and which I have now learnt to distrust so profoundly. I had to do it myself once, with an unmuzzled ferret scratching at the seat of my breeches, and a very anxious five minutes I had, for he was a ferret who was liable to use his teeth when his claws failed to clear the way. However he spared me, and the anxious conversation came to an end, and I was able to get up unscathed. I wish you all equal luck.

CHAPTER IX

COOKERY AND THE FINE ARTS

So far, in my efforts to show you what is your whole duty as a boy, I have dealt with the sterner and more savage side of life. But in this chapter I am going to make a great change, and try to kindle in your hearts that desire after polish and cultivation and refinement, which marks all the greatest men. Look at Richard of the Lion's Heart, for instance. Where will you find a better fighter or more thorough man ? And yet he would have been just as much ashamed and angry if anyone had told him that he could not make poetry, or sing a good song, as he would have been, had any question been raised about his fighting or hunting powers.

Bluff King Hal again, the husband of many wives, was very much a man, as far as love of sport went, but he, too, had a very polished side somewhere. And so I think that all you young fellows do greatly err, who think that only one side is worth cultivating. But let me not alarm you by this very serious commencement. I have other fish to fry. Yes, that's exactly what I wanted to tell you, how to fry fish, and other cookery ; for of all the fine arts, to my mind, cookery holds the first place, not that I like my dinner better than other men, but I like the making of it. So far I have rather taught you how to catch your hare. Now I wish to tell you how to cook him, and as you must catch him before you cook him, so I had to write all those hunting chapters, in order to enable me to work up to this chapter, which is to be the crown of my labours.

Now, in order to be a good cook, before all things it is necessary to cultivate the friendship of the real cook, as I think I observed in one of my earlier chapters. There are such a lot of things that you can get better from her than from anyone else. Let us take the ordinary sparrow, who has been caught by one of the many ways wherein I have endeavoured to instruct you. You have to pluck him first, unless you skin him, which is the easier plan, besides which it teaches you how to skin birds for stuffing. At any rate you've got to unfeather him, and if he's at all a big bird like a duck, as he may be, you must singe him to make a really smart dish of him. I'm not telling you all this at second hand : I've done every bit of it, and enjoyed it all, more than most things. The weakest part of that lovely book, " Tom Brown's School Days," is where they let their duck go to waste, just because it was a bother to pluck. A quarter of an hour would have been ample time to skin the beast and have him ready for roasting. I always wanted to re-write that page, and bring him to table all smoking hot, and stuffed with sage and onions. After getting off every scrap of feather somehow, then comes the cleaning, which we must not dwell upon beyond saying that it is not as bad as it sounds. At any rate, all good cooks do it thoroughly. I always held my bird under a tap for a minute. Keep the liver, and do things smartly ; a bad cook shirks these

N

details.   I always stuffed my sparrows with bread-crumbs and sage and onions, chopped small with my pocket-knife, to which stuffing, for variety's sake, I sometimes added the liver.   Otherwise I tucked it under one wing, where you find it in chickens.   Then you sew the breast up with a needle and thread.   I'd never have known so accurately about all this, if I had not been specially polite to one cook, who taught me.   But she was very strict otherwise and would not let me fry things in her kitchen ; so I had to go into the saddle-house, where there was always a fire to warm the green-house.   When the cook was in a good temper I had a frying-pan and a bit of dripping ; when she wasn't, I did without : but when we had a cook, whose bad temper I could rely on, I always smuggled away the bits of fat I had at dinner, which I hated, but had to eat unless I could surreptitiously cause them to vanish.

Now whether you have a cook who will allow you in the kitchen, or whether you have to go elsewhere, makes no real difference, except in the way of having things handy : there are still the same two ways of cooking a sparrow, depending on the presence or absence of a frying-pan, and I advise you to practise without, as you can't always rely on a cook's temper.   All you want is a plate, pepper, and some lard or cold fat, and a piece of string.   You tie the string to one of the hind-legs, and with your right hand dangle the bird in front of the fire.

If there is a nail handy all the better, for then you tie him up, and twist the string now and then and have your right hand free to apply pepper from time to time.   With your left hand you hold the plate under him to catch the gravy, having first melted the fat in the plate.   You want a spoon, which I forgot, and with it you keep on pouring the fat and gravy over the roasting bird, and soon he begins to smell delicious, so that you can hardly help beginning to eat him at once. I often wondered how cooks could ever help eating all the dinner that they were cooking ; I daresay they do eat some, just to see that it's all right. I should, I'm sure. When he's done, and you'll have to guess how long that takes, until you've had a lot of experience, you ought to put him on the plate in front of the fire to simmer and keep warm, while you do a bit of toast. You'll be lucky if you escape without some ashes tumbling in, but that can't be helped. One never seems to have hands enough for cooking. Then you take him in triumphantly to tea, and watch people begin to sniff and wonder where the roast partridges are. You generally offer your mother some, and even a sister sometimes, but they usually say " No."

If you find them getting into the habit of saying " Yes," you'll either have to do two or three, which is rather hard work, unless you have the frying-pan, or else you'll have to bring one up rather underdone, and with a cinder or two in the gravy, in which case they probably won't like it. It's not a bad thing to leave out the pepper in cooking them too, for then they don't either smell or taste so nice. You can do eels easily enough in this way, but you are almost obliged to have a frying-pan for other fish, as they tumble to bits. I was given a frying-pan of my own before long, which was a great help, though it was an awful bother to keep clean ; and when I had got that, I began to do buttered eggs, with sparrows' and starlings' eggs, unless, as sometimes happened, I found a place where a hen was laying wild in a hedge-bottom. You break them up in a mug, and beat the yolk and white all together with a fork, then pour them into the frying-pan, in which you have got a bit of butter, if possible, or melted fat, simmering, and stir them well about as they fry, pouring in a drop of

milk, if you can get it.   You've no idea, until you try,
what a ripping dish you can make, again with the help
of a little pepper, out of starlings' eggs and dripping,
over the saddle-room fire.   We used to have regular
feasts in there on winter evenings, sitting on the warm
pipes until they got too hot for comfort.   The delicious
time was just when you were not quite sure whether
the pipes were too hot or not, but it didn't last long.
We usually began with fish, if we'd managed to spear
any, or wire them ;   then buttered eggs, on the rare
occasions when we'd either found or been given a hen's
egg, then roast sparrows, or even a blackbird, and once
a pigeon, slain on the wing with a catapult by a lucky
shot (I hope the owner won't read this), and fried potatoes
to finish up on.   And for drink one of our many vintages,
which I'll have to talk about when I've done with cooking.

You can't say that that was a meal to be despised,
especially as it was all extra, and our real tea of bread
and butter and jam was still to come.   We met a dear
lady once at a proper indoor tea, who had heard of our
fame as cooks, and she strongly advised us to try a mouse,
because if we could only say it was real nice, it would
be so good for the poor to know that there was a cheap
dish ready to hand.   She seemed so much in earnest
that we did try.   We caught a fat one, and skinned him,
and he looked horribly ugly, but we stuck to our task,
for the sake of the poor, and got as far as half-roasting
him, but no amount of pepper could make us fancy that
he didn't smell, and we had to give him up.   We never
saw the lady again, which was perhaps as well, because
we had come to the conclusion that she had been making
game of us, and we weren't pleased with her, and meant
to tell her so, and there might have been ructions.   I'm
afraid that cooking is rather a lost art among boys
nowadays, which is a pity, as you may be cast up on a

desert island yet, and then what will you do ? There may be pepper trees handy, and gulls' eggs, and yams, and all the materials, and you'll starve, just because you don't know how to cook a dish. I know it's hard at school, as there is a prejudice in certain quarters against using the gas jet for cooking purposes. But you might at any rate practise at home, where all the materials are handy, and nobody to raise any frivolous objections.

But if boys are in danger of losing the art of cooking, there is no doubt that the talent is still there, only for want of practice it has been diverted towards the kindred branch of inventing dessert dishes. Strawberries and cream are almost out of fashion, and the really correct dish to invite your friends to partake of is squashed bananas, rather tending to over-ripeness, well worked up with rich cream, and a dash of strawberry ice on the top, served up in slop-basins. There is no doubt that the inventive talent is there still, but what a change from my young days, when I used to invite my friends in, and give them curry, made in a coffee-pot over the gas, of tinned meat chopped small, and hard-boiled eggs and curry powder ; and then when that was served, my fag had to wash out the pot, and coffee was brewed and drunk, and the banquet ended with plain pears and apples, not always bought, because there was an orchard handy, well guarded, so that it was the owner's fault if any apples went astray, as they sometimes did. Perhaps the modern banquet of mixed biscuits and banana-cream is more æsthetic, but mine was good. .

Now to turn to drinks. Invention, in extreme youth, ran no further than an everlasting bottle of liquorice and water, rather simple perhaps, but less harmful than some port wine I drank at Cambridge, and much the same in colour and flavour : but in later life we became very great adepts in the art of brewing. Dried cowslip flowers, if well dried, and not packed too tight, make excellent tea right up to Christmas, but as this always struck us as a sort of tame tea-party drink, our ambitions soared higher towards cowslip wine and elderberry wine. The thing is to get a good strong decoction of the flowers or berries, by boiling or just soaking, and then bottle it with a couple of raisins, and half-a-dozen grains of rice, and bury it deep for a month or two. The rice and raisins make it ferment, and if the bottle doesn't burst under ground, the result is almost intoxicating, when it isn't too nasty to drink. The worst of it is a certain tendency to cause pains under the pinafore, so that, except when we happened to broach an unusually success-ful bottle, the drinking part of our banquets was a series of experiments, often ending in a demand for plain water. But just now and then we came on what we considered a real fine drink, so that the experiments were kept up for many years : the misfortune is that, as we never knew just what accident had made the one bottle a success, I cannot give you any exact instructions ; only a general exhortation to brew hard, and never drink too much, if there is any doubt as to the soundness of the liquor, which rule may be worth remembering also in your later life.

I should like to go further into the whole question of " self-help " in matters of eating and drinking, but I hope that I have said enough to show what a wide field lies open for cultivation in this direction. You may meet with a certain amount of opposition ; you may even be driven to make a small bonfire in the wilds, and to wrap your game in lumps of clay, or bury it in holes and make the fire on the top. During a certain memorable time of persecution under an alien cook, I was driven to all these shifts, and though there is a certain wild charm about them, smacking of the backwoods and a trapper's life, I can't conscientiously say that the results were ever exactly what I hoped for. Things generally came out underdone, even the potatoes and apples that I buried in the ashes, or else roasted to a cinder. I found the oven very hard to regulate. And once I found, to my horror, that I had made my fire in rather close proximity to a stack, and had to extinguish it in a great hurry. I'd rather a narrow escape of getting into bad trouble then —even a life of imprisonment hovered before my distracted gaze. So look round carefully before you make a fire, if you are ever driven into the wilds. But whatever the difficulties and dangers that lie in your way, unless they come from a quarter that you neither can nor ought to disregard, do not be diverted from acquiring such store of knowledge as may one day be your safeguard in the hour of starvation, and from so polishing the more refined side of your character, that you may shine even in the most brilliant society.

Now for another facet of the gem. It is the duty of every boy to cultivate the talent for music, which has been given to all, and which often is only evidenced by the desire to whistle. I don't mean to exhort you to learn to play the piano, though one valse and two polkas learnt by heart are possessions that you will never regret. I still do a lot of trade with the three that I thoroughly mastered in my boyhood, and can play no others. Many is the country pub or small lodging-house whose gloomy atmosphere has been brightened by the sweet strains that my fingers have produced from some venerable piano. And many the drinks of an enthusiastic audience that I have had to refuse. I speak in no spirit of boastfulness. I *have* heard better pianists than myself. But I learnt those three tunes by the sweat of my brow, and amidst continual discouragement, and I want to encourage you to do the same. Still the piano will always be regarded by boys as an instrument of torture, and the view is so widely spread, even amongst elder people, that I feel a certain modest hesitation in urging you to open it. It is with a wilder orchestra that I have to deal. Very few boys nowadays seem to me to know how to make a whistle. Willow is the best wood, then sycamore ; but almost any wood will serve the purpose. Get a nice piece about as thick as your thumb, about three or four inches long, with at least two inches at one end free from all blemishes in the bark. (It is no good trying to make a whistle unless the leaves are on the tree.) Shape this smooth end like an ordinary whistle, as in the illustration, and two inches from the end, cut the bark round in a ring. Wet the whole end down to the ring in your mouth or elsewhere, according to taste, and tap gently all over with a smooth knife handle, not neglecting any corner of it. If you get impatient, and tap too hard, the bark will split. After some two minutes of this gentle tapping (keeping the bark wet all the time), try to twist the bark round the least bit, and if it won't move, keep on wetting and tapping, until at last it goes with a little sort of delicious crack. If you have twisted too hard, you will most probably split. It only just ought to move from its foundations, so to speak. And if again you have neglected to tap any corner, that corner will stick, and spoil your job. You are nearly certain to have to learn through failure. But supposing that you have just made the bark go with that little crack, now slip it carefully off the end, leaving the bare and shining wood to work on. You will see the nick in the wood, where you cut a chip out of the bark on the top, to make the hole for the air to come out of. Begin cutting carefully here, till you have excavated, as in the second illustration. Then shave a little slice off at the place marked A, to blow through. Cut off too little rather than too much, for you can easily shave off a bit more, if the wind doesn't go in properly, but if you cut off too much, the whole thing is done for, and may be thrown away. The longer you make the main cutting, the deeper the tone of the whistle. But you'll have to be very careful of your fingers. I still shiver when I remember how that knife went into the side of my left fore-finger, time after time ; I can still count five distinct marks, left by extra deep gashes.

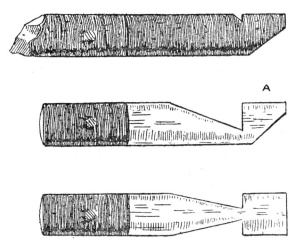

A

To trespass into the domain of medicine for a moment, I always kept a lot of dry puff balls, such as one picks up in the autumn pastures, and was seldom without one, among the miscellaneous collection that crammed my various pockets. There is nothing like a bit of the brown woolly stuff out of the middle of one of these to stop bleeding. It is far better than cobwebs, and if you *know* that you have one in your pocket, easier to find, on the whole, in a hurry.

To return : when you have thoroughly finished your wood-carving, slip the bark on again carefully, having first given the wood a good lick, and blow with all your might, and a wonderfully fine and piercing whistle should reward your efforts. It is well to make two or three, as people are liable to say, however polite they are, that one gets monotonous. After all, the pleasure is more in the making of them than in their continuous use. They don't last long, even if you keep them in water, as the bark withers and cracks. The culminating point of the art is to make a double one, as shown in picture three, blowing two notes at once. And it is in making this that you will get most of your bad cuts, as the knife goes through the thin part.

Perhaps the best instrument of all for whistling is your own fingers, but I can't teach you how to do it. I can do it personally in every imaginable way, but it is not to be taught. The easiest way is with the middle- and fore-finger of each hand, if your mouth will hold them all, pressed close to each other, at about such an angle as will be made if you join your little fingers, which are folded down along with the fourth finger. How far they go into your mouth you must judge for yourself, and your mouth then goes into as near the ordinary position for whistling as you can get it. Then it is merely a matter of practice, and when you have mastered that position, you can try with each pair of fingers in turn, the thumbs being the hardest, and the two little fingers the easiest. Last of all you crook your fore-finger pretty tight, with the nail against the thumb, and put most of it into your mouth and blow. It is a pretty and graceful art, not suited for ladies' drawing-rooms, though I can play " The British Grenadiers " on my fingers, but really very useful in the country, when you want to fetch some-body from a long way off.

To complete your orchestra, you will want squeaks of all sorts. The blade of grass between your thumbs is too well known to require description, but there are three others that I ought to tell you of. Cut off three inches of a dandelion stalk (the flower stalk, I mean), and at the lower and broader end cut a slit longwise, with the point of your knife, about three-quarters of an inch long, beginning a quarter of an inch from the bottom. Put the bottom into your mouth, till the whole slit is well covered by your lips, and blow, and a pleasing sound will result, but a nasty taste. Then take an ordinary white-flowering nettle and cut it off just above the lowest bunch of flowers, and about two and a half inches below them. Make a nick close to the flowers as you did in the dandelion, and use it in the same way. There is no nasty taste, and the note is a finer and more attractive one, but the flowers tickle the back of your mouth in an awkward way.

Perhaps the nicest of all is a bit of good fat oat-straw, cut off just above a joint at one end, and about the same length as the other two, but instead of making a slit longwise, you cut half through the straw with a sharp blade, about an inch and a quarter above the joint, and then turn the blade and run it downwards nearly to the joint. Use like the others, and you will be pleased. You can manage as many as three, if you are clever, of different tones. I forgot to say that there is a more lasting form of whistle to be made by taking a piece of elder wood, and pushing the pith out with a skewer, after cutting it into whistle shape, and then fitting in a plug of plain wood to stop up the bottom altogether, and another plug carefully carved, with room for a blowing channel. It is a difficult piece of carpentering, but very interesting.

I have still one more musical instrument, which completes the orchestra very nicely. You get an old thimble and put it on your finger, and rub it on a rough stone till you have worn the top away. When this is neatly done, get a bit of old parchment from somebody, and tie it tightly round the bigger end. Make a pin-hole through the middle of the parchment, and through this pass a good horsehair, tying something on to the end which will draw inside the thimble, to prevent it coming through the hole in the parchment. Lick your finger and thumb, and, holding the thimble tightly in your left hand, jerk your damp fingers lightly down the horsehair. This charming instrument will enable you to imitate the songs of those matchless songsters, the partridge and jackdaw, with some exactitude, and will be audible in any band. I said it would complete the orchestra, but if you want a droning bass, like the bagpipes, to make a sort of background, cut a lath of wood, about a foot long and an inch and a half wide, and as thick as two half-crowns, if you have them to measure with. If not, borrow them. Fine down the edges, and cut little notches all down both sides. Then bore a hole about an inch from one end and pass a piece of string through, a yard or more in length. If you whirl the wood round your head as fast as you can, at the full length of the string, you will get a fine humming sound. When you have thoroughly mastered all these instruments, no one will be able to cast it in your teeth that you are no musician, and you will be able to command an orchestra that will make the nightingales in the wood blush, and hush their minstrelsy for very shame. I advise you to play in the woods, not so much to shame the nightingales, as because music is not always properly appreciated in the home circle, and to compensate for their not casting in your teeth lack of music, they may cast other things, not greatly caring whether they take you in the teeth, or in some other part of your person. I should hate to think that I had made you unpopular.

That, I think, finishes what I consider to be the two most important branches of a boy's artistic education. I am not prepared to consider drawing, because it seems to me to be either given or denied to us at birth. No amount of instruction would have taught me to draw much difference between a horse or a cow, except by putting two spikes, to represent horns, on the head of the latter. But there were many small ways in which I endeavoured to prevent people being able to call me a philistine and a runagate, and I should like to mention them briefly, to give you some sort of idea as to how one can fill up one's leisure time, without necessarily getting into mischief.

Gardening, I should say, comes first, and I do hope that you will be able to beg a small slab of Mother Earth's broad breast to delve in, though it is not absolutely necessary. I had my own proper little garden, but I loved better a bit of stolen ground on a stream bank. It was only about a square yard of sloping ground, but I claimed the water-way too. The stream was barely two feet wide, but I dammed it carefully with large flints and clay, and made a waterfall. I also excavated a sort of backwater out of the bank, which served as an aquarium for tadpoles when it was duly fenced in. This was my pet retreat, when world-weariness came over me, as I suppose it comes over everyone at times, and here I planted my choicest bulbs and cuttings. It was a fragile affair, that little plot of ground, and very liable to land-slips. In fact a heavy shower was usually fatal, for the soil had been made so fine, by being constantly put through an old sieve, that a good breeze even would remove it. But it was very dainty when freshly made, with its partitions of shells, and single snowdrops, and little cuttings of wallflower, which never had time to root. It may sound a small trifle, but I date back to it all my immense love of gardening, which has so often stood as a buffer between me and sorrow, when even the joys of cookery and of music failed to win me back to happiness. The bigger garden in the midst of civilisation was also dear to my heart in a way, because it was liable to visits of inspection from headquarters, and consequent criticism, which criticism always gave me a chance of total reconstruction, and reconstruction was what I really loved. I did not learn much science, but I do realise thoroughly now what a lot flowers will stand in the way of being transplanted in full blossom. My ambition in this garden was to have a fountain in the middle for sticklebacks. I could manage a small jet of water with some old indiarubber tubing and a bucket in a neighbouring tree, but the water would never remain in the pond, and so the goldfish, sticklebacks I mean, had to be removed elsewhere. I loved this garden well, as I say, and if you can get no better one, take such, but make it your own to experimentalise on, and don't let any adverse criticism turn you from your purpose, for you will learn best by personal experience.

Wet days were always a trial, till I learnt a few parlour-tricks to practise, which may very reasonably be called accomplishments. I should like to talk about fretwork, but it rather comes among indoor games, which someone else is going to take in hand, I believe. My business is just to tread upon the tails of everyone, who either has written or is going to write, about proper pursuits like cricket and hunting ; to lay a good foundation to your character, so to speak. Therefore I must leave fretwork alone, and talk about things that are less known, but equally necessary for the boy or man who would be perfect.

Most of the things I have to mention can only be learnt by real hard practice, and are therefore the more valuable for a wet day. I met a brother-in-law of Nansen in Norway, who could place an ordinary walking stick on the space between the first and second joint of his thumb, on the outside, not the inside, and could keep it there, without the help of his other hand, just by swinging his arm backwards and forwards. I have been trying for two years now to do it, and have got so far as only to break something once in every three tries, but, if I had begun young, I can feel that I could have done it, and I do want to, so badly. It is all a question of accurate balance and shifting the thumb as the stick swings, so that the pressure comes alternately just above and just below the centre, and on the backward journey, when it looks as if the thumb must leave the stick in mid air, curling the joint below the nail round it in a queer sort of way.

Another good stick trick is rather easier. Bend your left elbow, holding the hand up in the air, and measure with a stick from the tip of the middle finger to a point just below the elbow joint. Then with your right hand clasp the stick just below this point, so that the *back* of your right hand faces your body. Clench all the fingers tight, with the thumb folded over the others, and put into your mouth the end of the stick which was at the tip of your middle finger. It is easy if you slacken the grasp of the fingers, or let the thumb come straight, but not easy when the hold is well maintained.

One more of the hundreds of these tricks I may select to give you employment. Take a handkerchief, and wrap the two ends round your two hands, so that your hands are not more than ten inches apart when the handkerchief is fully stretched. Hold tight, and put the handkerchief over your head and down behind your back. The secret is as follows. Hold your right hand still, and bring the left round in front of it, with the handkerchief passing *underneath*, continue the left round the bend of your right elbow, and so your left wrist will pass over your head, and all will come straight.   Learn to do it quickly before you show off before anyone.

When times were slack, we went in for glass melting. There was a bit of plantation near the house, where old bottles and broken glass had been thrown for generations. For this we used to grub among the dead leaves and rubbish with sticks, when the surface supply got scarce, as it soon did : finally it took two of us a good hour to get the necessary supply.   Window glass was no use. This glass we threw into the furnace that boiled the pigs' food, etc., and after about half-an-hour, little trickles of glass used to drop down underneath, and if you laid hold of these with a thick wet glove, and pulled carefully, you could get out as much as a yard of glass, as fine as a hair, attached to the little pear-shaped drop that had originally fallen.   And in the morning, when the cinders were taken out, there were huge cakes of cinder, cemented together with great solid bubbles of melted glass, which made most ornamental edgings and decorations for our garden.   I finally made quite an elegant rockery over half my garden, composed almost entirely of this stuff. I suppose now that it looked like a rubbish heap, but I thought it mighty fine at the time, and I have still a tendency to pull a great slice of my garden to pieces and make a rockery.   It is most fascinating work, this architecture of stones and earth, and I fancy my skill now, almost as much as I did in those olden days, and probably am just as much derided as I was then, only people don't give their opinions quite so freely as of old. Still, I never let my brothers mock at my efforts to be artistic.

While the glass was melting in the furnace, we occupied our time partly in picking out and eating the tiny potatoes that were boiling for the pigs. These were the only potatoes that I ever really cared for. And partly in melting stolen scraps of lead in an iron shovel, and running them into the tops of old buttons to make medals, or into clay moulds, which we had previously constructed with what skill we could muster among us, to represent various objects. That clay was a great joy in idle moments. Jolly clean dirt to knead, and make bricks and marbles, and even ambitious statues of men and animals, which always came to pieces in the baking.

Also we used to have great slinging contests. You can throw, with some accuracy, a good-sized pellet of damp clay from the end of a strong hazel wand about a yard long, or rather less, if you stick it on pretty tight. Our favourite target was an old disused pigeon-house on the top of the stables, showing four openings. To hit the house at all was one mark. The openings counted three each, and the little ball on the top was worth five, and when we were in good practice we made that old pigeon-house look as if giant martins had begun to build their nests. Looking back into old days, it seems to me that, if I had had more time, and had wanted any more hobbies than I am possessed of already, these early pursuits of boyhood made an excellent foundation for scientific glass blowing, and modelling in wax, either of which fascinating pursuits I could have taken up with joy, as the result of my early experiments in these directions.

And also I might have become a great maker of fireworks. When we got any spare gunpowder we concocted gunpowder paste, which was made into a cone-shaped volcano and allowed to dry slowly. Then on a dark evening we did fireworks, with two of these to let off on the gravel walk, as set pieces, and bits of dry touchwood out of the old poplar stumps, tied to pieces of string, and whirled round our heads when well ignited, and hurled into the air, for squibs and rockets and catherine wheels. How we chased one another through the shrubberies with these whirling fragments of glowing wood, while the blackbirds fled affrighted from the laurels ! Jolly days, when amusement could be got out of such things, but I believe I could enjoy chasing a man now with a good touchwood spinner, to make a great circle of fire round my head.

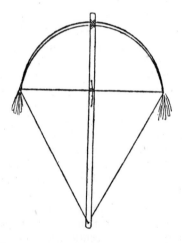

I am glad to see that kites are coming into fashion again, even among grown-up people. Boys are still professedly scornful of them, and if the fashion does not spread downwards from age to youth, then I must write the conclusion of this chapter for the old folk. For I can never forget the joys of my first kite. How I took a lath of four feet and a good cane, and lashed the latter by the centre to the top of the former, and then string and paper did the rest. I think I substituted thin calico for paper eventually, as being more lasting, but strong paper will do. The sketch will show you the framework. Then you bore two holes, above and below the centre of the lath, or rather higher, and pass a string through both, fastening it with a strong knot at the back, not drawing it too tight. To this the main string is attached, and the tail is fastened tightly through or round the bottom of the lath. What joy to make that tail, with its twists of paper at intervals of a foot and the bunch of hay at the bottom. I always gave my kites wings, generally of pink tissue paper cut into thin strips, and fastened in two bunches at the ends of the cane. And the paper or calico I adorned with stars and stripes and other devices, such as my artistic taste suggested. I wonder who was the original inventor of the kite, whether he cut holes through pieces of paper, and passed them over the stick to which the string was tied, and sent them fluttering up to the kite aloft, with insulting messages and stern orders to behave itself? He was a clever man, and history has acted with unfair partiality in not handing down his name to posterity. I would have learnt it much more willingly than that of men who discovered such everyday truths, as that the sun does not walk round the earth, and that the blood does run about your body. I should have thought that anyone who ever cut his finger, decently and like a gentleman, would have made the latter discovery easily enough, without Dame History making such a fuss over it. Whoever he was, let him know that one blessing, at all events, rests upon his memory. And if glass melting showed traces of a possible rival to Salviati, and the clay-moulding of an apt disciple of Polycletus (and does not even the Latin Grammar praise his statues?), surely in flying kites there is evidence that there might have been another victim to balloons besides André, and that there even yet may be the inventor of the ideal flying-machine. What a future there is in

front of the boy who can bring all his youthful hobbies
to their logical conclusion and consummation. I'm afraid
you won't be able to develop them all, but stick to them
till you find out which is the right one, and whether you
win renown for cookery, or music, or pottery, or sculpture,
or a flying-machine, I shall feel that I have not written
in vain. Vagabonds at heart I would have you, for
your own happiness, but that a vagabond should be also
an artistic vagabond is the best of all, for so alone does
he really rise above the level of the Tramp.

I have said nothing of Poetry, but may I venture to
give you one specimen to prove that I have even attacked
this lesser art, this younger sister of Cookery.

Come forth, come forth : the spring to thee is calling :
    The lapwing cries his love o'er moor and hill :
The skylark's notes from heaven to earth are falling :
    And in the hedgerow nods the daffodil.

Come forth, come forth : the summer's fiery glances
    Bid thee come sleep beneath the pine tree's shade.
Where the glad streamlet through the bracken dances,
    And the tall foxglove blushes in the glade.

Come forth, come forth : the autumn mists are creeping
    About the garden where the robin sings.
The spider in his dewy web is sleeping,
    And to his hoard his nuts the squirrel brings.

Lie still and rest : the winter winds are wailing :
    The sparrow puffs his feathers on the tree,
While sullen clouds o'er sullen skies are trailing.
    What can the dead earth tell to thee or me ?

CHAPTER X

THE YOUNG CAMPAIGNER

THERE is a certain solemnity about a last chapter, which might seem to call for a greater weightiness of diction than has hitherto, I fear, been apparent in these pages. But if there be such a need, let us postpone it till the nearer sight of the end causes us to slacken our paces and dally over the last few pages of our acquaintanceship. Before the actual moment of parting comes, I have somewhat to say to you on the subject of the joys of life in general, and camping out in particular.

As to the latter, I have rather stolen the best of my experiences to introduce the sea to your notice, but I hope to find other stores to draw from. For, as I daresay you have realised, wild life has irresistible charms for me, and these charms force themselves upon a man's notice nowhere so intensely as when he casts off the bonds of civilisation, as represented by bedrooms, collars, baths and kitchens, and reverts for a while to a state of primitive savagery, sleeping where the ground is softest and nature provides the curtains, bathing wherever he can find a pool or stream to wallow in, dressing in the untidiest minimum, and last of all joys, cooking for himself, or partaking, if his early training has failed to include cookery, of such homely fare as the country pub has to offer.   If it were given into my hands to organise Utopia, the first law that I would make would be, that all fathers, under sixty years of age, should, for the space of one fortnight in the summer months, disappear from the world with their sons and no more baggage than they could themselves carry, and on their return produce a certificate that they had not slept under a roof for more than two nights of that period.   And if in this book I have made any statement of my views, which I felt sure would win to my side the hearts of all boys, however much it might estrange from me the sympathy of their fathers, I feel confident that here is such a statement.   But I am in a way serious in making such a statement, for under no circumstances does friendship ripen so quickly, never do its bonds rivet themselves with so durable a clasp, as when two folk elect for a while to trust themselves to the keeping of Dame Nature.   And if this is good for a pair of casual acquaintances, much more is it good for father and son.   And if you plead rheumatism on the one side, and a tendency to catch cold on the other, I can only say, " Pick a spell of dry weather, and I don't think it will hurt you."

The luxurious style of course is to take a tent, as we did to those sandhills in Lincolnshire, but it never quite strikes me as the real thing.   What I call the real thing is to go with just a warm jersey, and to tuck yourself away somewhere under the loose straw round a stack, or under a pile of bracken, or in a woodshed for protection against the cool air, which you are bound to feel in the small hours of the morning.   I can't profess to have done it a great deal; I can count on my two hands the nights on which I have slept out in this way. But I have done enough to wish greatly that I had done it more, and I can certainly say that I never felt any the worse for it, and enjoyed the unfettered freedom of it more than I can describe. But on the whole I am afraid that, until you are your own masters, you will have to be content with day work.

I knew a pair of boys once, whose whole spare time was spent camping out in the wilds. They made themselves an underground den in a wood, fairly roomy, by dint of excavating and roofing with turf and branches, and here they spent pretty nearly the whole of their spare time, being mostly engaged in cookery, with a small spirit stove, of the most varied description. They had shelves and store cupboards dug in the walls of their den, and provisions of many kinds kept in tins, for fear of squirrels invading the place, or rats; also a big thunderstorm would make a flood. I had the honour of being invited once to inspect the house, and partake of light refreshment. My hosts took with them a cottage loaf and a tin of butter. We crept in, like foxes into an earth, and I found myself in the dark, and was requested to keep squatting for fear I'd knock the roof off. Three candle ends soon lighted up what I may politely describe as a spacious dwelling. There was room at any rate for three people to sit on little piles of fir branches, with a space in the middle for cooking. The walls were honeycombed with burrows, out of one of which came the spirit lamp, out of another a box of sardines, out of another a tin of potted meat. Then a biscuit tin out of a larger hole with a fine piece of bacon inside it, a tin of preserved milk out of another, pepper, salt, forks and spoons out of others. The walls were also adorned with tin mugs and a frying-pan. It was the most amazing product of the ingenuity

of two boys, who had determined to live wild.   They
said that they had got the idea from Homer, whose works
were being forced upon their notice during that special
term.   They were pleased with the way in which the
heroes despised perforated bedsteads, and after partaking
all day of immeasurable meats and sweet wine, just lay
them down and slept on the beach, or wherever they
happened to be, until rosy-fingered dawn woke them.
They had all the necessary meats, and a tin of cocoa for
sweet wine, and I thought it would be better to ask no
questions about the sleeping on the beach.   I know, if
the idea had come to me in my youth to do such a thing,
I'd have contrived to get away from my perforated bed-
stead for one night, even at the risk of my neck, and
would have slept in my den, whatever might have been
the cost.   When they talked about the beach and the
sleeping out, I just fancied that I detected a note of anxiety
in their voices, a sort of unspoken prayer that I would
ask no awkward questions, so I held my tongue, and put
forth my hands upon the victuals.   First the cocoa was
brewed in the tin mugs, and then down came the frying-
pan, and the smell of the frizzling bacon filled the whole
house, and floated out into the recesses of the wood.
Toast alone was wanting, and my hosts apologised for
the shortcomings of their establishment, with a certain
air of conscious pride, as much as to say that there wasn't
a great deal else that they couldn't produce.   I dived
into all the cupboards and inspected all the boxes.   They
watched me with a smile, and when I had done, they
said, " No, sir, we haven't got any : we don't use them,"
Then I knew what I had been looking for, and was rather
ashamed at being caught suspecting my hosts of storing
cigarettes.   I am afraid the house got very hot, in spite
of a carefully concealed air hole in the roof, so I did not
stay long after my meal.   I was not allowed to put any-

thing away, for fear I'd put it in the wrong cupboard, but at my earnest request I was permitted to clean my own mug, and to have a second scrub at the frying-pan. It was a most extraordinary meal in a most extraordinary house, and I came away feeling as if I'd been visiting a very primitive but tidy tribe of savages, with extraordinarily nice manners.

Now, whether I shall get hauled over the coals for putting such ideas into your heads, I don't know. It is more than likely that I shall shortly receive a furious postcard, or an agitated four-page letter, from a father or mother, saying, " Where are my lost boys, you evil man ? It's your fault, so come and find them." Then I will reply by telegram, regardless of the expense, " Be of good cheer, sir or madam ; if I am responsible for their absence, I can assure you that they are doing no evil and will come back all in good time, much the better for their outing, with their tails behind them, and if you choose to twist or otherwise maltreat these tails, I shall think it very unkind of you. Please to remember that even great King Nebuchadnezzar himself was once seized with this feeling, and refused to cut his nails or to live in his palace, and that he came back all right and found his kingdom still waiting for him, in days when kingdoms were insecure. So it must have been counted unto him for good. Therefore deal gently with your little wanderers, and accept, not my apologies, but my hearty congratulations on having so right minded and excellent a pair of sons." That will run to quite a decent-sized telegram, not the shabby sort of things that people vex my soul with, only half worded, so that you can generally construe them in quite six different ways. I hope the meaning of mine is quite clear.

It has been my habit in the past to take various of my young friends, on various pretexts, down to the wilds of

the New Forest, on certain holidays which we are allowed
to enjoy in this Academy. Entomology was the generally
accepted pretext, and when I first took the job in hand,
it was considered etiquette to show me, at the end of
the day, at least a grasshopper shut up in a bottle, as a
proof of zeal and entomological capacity. You see, we
were called the Entomological Society in very large letters.
But I am afraid that this formality dropped after a while,
when it was found that I, and those above me, regarded
the desire for a day's liberty in the wilds as a sufficient
excuse. I easily weeded out the unworthy specimens,
and flatter myself that a more blameless crew, in the
more important sense of the word, never broke through
the smaller ties of civilisation. I regret to say that
pressure of business has, of late years, compelled me to
sever my connection with " The Entomological Society,"
so that I shall be revealing no personal secrets, if I relate
to you a few of our more esoteric experiences. And I
can do so best in the form of personal narrative. I asked
two of the choicest and most select products of my teaching
to dinner ; I might almost go so far as to call them the
ultimate perfection of my training, so thoroughly had
they imbibed the spirit of my doctrine. And if you
could see them now, I cannot think that you could do
otherwise than accept a system which has resulted in
two so stately and well-balanced citizens of that empire
on which the sun never sets. They are in themselves a
refutation of the Yankee calumny, that it wouldn't do to
leave us in the dark. After dinner I demanded an account
of their day, and it ran somewhat as follows :—

" When we got out of the train, sir, we provisioned
the ship with a store of squished flies (*i.e.*, biscuits with
squashed currants) and had a couple of bottles of ginger-
beer each. Then we went along the road till we got
opposite the police-station, where we saw a couple of

mokes. They didn't seem to belong to anyone, so we got on to them and had a ride. Then we came to a ditch, and as one would jump it and the other wouldn't, we let the one that wouldn't go home (I hope it ever got there) and took it in turns to jump the ditch till he wouldn't jump any more, so we let him go too ; but we wished we hadn't, as we soon found a lot of wild pigs, and might have tried some pig-sticking. However, we settled that whoever caught a pig first by the hind-leg should have two of the other man's squished flies. We each of us tumbled about twenty times, sir, and we couldn't catch hold, enough to say that we had got one, and at last we nearly got into trouble, because, in coming out of some bushes, we all ran against an artist who was sketching, and upset the thing he had his picture on, and one of the pigs nearly got between his legs. He was so angry, and wouldn't listen to us, that we had to go away. And at last we drove the pigs on to a bridge over a big stream, and made sure that we'd got them, because Hugh was at one end and I was at the other; but suddenly they all began to jump into the water, and one little chap had to swim, and we were afraid he'd cut his throat, so I jumped in too, and helped him out. And I might have got his hind-leg, but it wouldn't have been playing the game, sir, would it ? So we agreed to stop, and have our own squished flies ourselves. We were badly hungry and wished we'd brought more, but we found a shoal of little fish in one corner of the stream, and managed to catch a lot in our straw hats. (Parents ask me why a straw lasts for so short a time !) So we made a bonfire and toasted them on pointed sticks, and they *were* good, sir. And we got some water out of the stream and made cocoa in our jam crock, which we always take. Then we were so hot that we thought we'd like a bath, so we undressed and found a place where we could get a bit of a swim, and we stayed there an hour. And when we'd just dried and got our shirts on, we saw another moke, and we thought it would be rare larks to catch him and ride him, sort of extra bare-backed you know, sir. But the heather was so prickly to run in that he got away, and we'd made ourselves so hot that we had to have another swim, and by the time we'd got our things on, it was time to come home, if we wanted to get any tea at the pub, and that's about all we did, sir."

After that elegant recital of adventure, I was a bit anxious on all future occasions, not knowing exactly what my flock might take it into their heads to do, and I went about Lyndhurst on such days, studiously avoiding my friends and acquaintances, for fear of a quarrel. But I never got hauled over the coals once, which only shows how indulgent the world is to the young, as long as they do their bits of mischief in a natural and cheerful way. I did think I was in for trouble once, when I met an obviously excited rustic, who stopped me with the ominous words—

" Be you the gent that's in charge of these young gentlemen down here ? "

There was no room to fly, so I said I was. He told me that one of them had been bitten by an adder, and had obviously gone mad, because he had come to their cottage and asked for a harmonium. I thought it sounded serious, but it occurred to me that the " harmonium " was probably " ammonia," as the young man knew something about chemistry. At any rate I went in pursuit, and soon came across one of my flock chasing a herd of swine violently along the road in the hot sun. Of him I asked who'd been bitten by an adder, and to my amazement he replied that he was the victim. I made some rather forcible remarks on the folly of a man with snake-bite on him racing about in the hot sun and spreading

the poison through his system. His defence was that he
thought the way to cure the bite of a cobra was to tie
a man to a dog-cart and keep him running, and that, as
he couldn't find a cart, he had started a pig-hunt. I
made him show me the place, and his whole hand was
swollen and livid, as if you had bruised it with a big
hammer. I made a sling, filled him with strong brandy
and water, gave him to a guard, and wired for a nurse
to meet the train at Winchester. He was sick all the way
home, and in bed for ten days, the livid bruise extending
along all the muscles of his arm and down his right side,
but he was none the worse in the end. It seems that he
prided himself on his skill in catching adders by the back
of the neck, and had often done it both here and at home,
but this one was too quick for him. It is not the kind
of skill that I should advise you to cultivate, as you are
bound to make a mistake sooner or later, and then you
get more or less the worst of it.

You see now I hope that, when I take my young friends
out for a walk, I am not unreasonably haunted by a dread
of what may happen. People say, " How nice to be out
with a lot of young folks : you'll never grow old ! "
I smile enigmatically, and stroke the top of my head,
where the wool once sprouted, and think to myself that
I have some idea as to the cause which has smoothed it
all away. Only last Ladysmith Day, one of my young
friends, with the help of a pal, tied a flag to the highest
chimney of my rather lofty house, with a very steep roof.
To do this he had to get out of a window, with a sheer
drop on to asphalte of forty or fifty feet, catch hold of
a gutter, get his friend to stand on the window ledge
and hoist him up, and on the return journey, slide down
the roof, stop at the gutter, dangle down, and get his
friend to haul him in. For a wonder the gutter was a
strong one, and stood the strain, and they are both alive

now ; but there is a very special Providence that watches over boys when their proper guardians are out of the way for a moment, as I was then, watching the rest of my flock.

Musical instruments were in great request on that day of enthusiasm. There was a fiddle, whose owner took it out for a little exercise. Getting tired of it, and wanting to wave a flag, he made an exchange with a friend, who was giving vent to his feelings with a flag tied to the end of his best trout rod. The fiddle was reduced to two strings by this time, but tune was unessential, as long as there was noise, and the friend sawed through the remaining strings, and then beat upon the back with the bow. When the bow gave way in the ordinary course of events, he passed the remainder of poor Stradivarius on to a casual acquaintance, who beat it to death on anything that came handy, other fellows' heads and that sort of thing, so that its sorrows were at an end. The fishing rod died also in detachments, and two parents were duly applied to, to make good the loss, and I suppose, if the history of the tragedy was made clear to them, paid up like men, and wished they were young again. Perhaps their own consciences weren't altogether void of offence. We heard some strange stories down here of what aged and respectable parents did in London and elsewhere.

One wants a very strong and perhaps rather distorted sense of humour thoroughly to appreciate boys. You see fun lurking in such odd corners, my young friends. I often have to smile, when I know I ought to scold. There was a sailor brother once, who came to stay with his brother, the schoolmaster, and being a handy man, was set to weed the garden. He put on a pair of old bags over his ample person, which bags had been ornamented, very likely by his own hands, with a fine and conspicuous patch, in the place where patches generally grow. Him, stooping over his work, Master Tommy espied, and was luckily heard to mutter to himself, " Oh for my catapult ! " He would have got it too, and used it, with a fine disregard of all consequences to himself and others—and they would have been severely painful in both cases, for he was a very accurate shot, and sailors are not lacking in temper, and have supple wrists, which put a little draw on to the stroke of the stick, just that little bit of drag which tests the skin of the recipient— but, luckily as I say, he was overheard, and the tragedy was averted, and Master Tommy had to content himself with making a spirited sketch in water colours. But I know that he felt in his little heart that he had been baulked of his lawful prey, and hardly treated, and the fact that the sailor bought the picture for a handsome price, as a thank-offering for his merciful escape, I suppose, did not altogether wipe away the memory of a wasted oppor- tunity. That is to my mind a very fair sample of a boy's sense of humour, and if you cannot appreciate it, certainly when others are the victims of it, and possibly even when you are the sufferer yourself, I should advise you to observe boys from a distance.

Of course I don't mean to say for a moment that the sufferer ought to be so amused as not to take vengeance. Tommy does not like the vengeance at the time, but he expects it, and the complete joy of his retrospect is marred, if the incident is not rounded off with a licking. I believe that both the actors in this last tableau are alive, and if this meets their eye, I crave their pardon for here sketching the scene, to illustrate my doctrines. The lack of respect for the feelings of others is greatly manifested, and too often, in a boy's dealings with animals, but it seldom runs to brutality, as it is liable to do in their dealings with their elders. They always realise, though rather late sometimes, that while the latter either can, or ought to, defend themselves, the former are at their mercy ; so that when they make their rival frogs jump, and go on jumping, till one has to give in from sheer exhaustion, they are usually sorry for it afterwards, and feel that it was rather bad luck on the poor beasts, and their hearts are eventually softened.

I asked two of my friends only the other day what they had been doing, as they seemed, by a look in their eyes and their somewhat dishevelled appearance, to have been having a good time.   They replied, " Rabbit races." This sounded interesting, so I pursued the subject further. Do you know how to find young rabbits in the wilds ? They are generally in quite a shallow hole.   And when the doe leaves them for a while, she covers up the hole with earth and stamps it down smooth and level.   In June you may go out anywhere, where there are plenty of bunnies, and see these smooth patches of soil, with nothing growing on them.   You would pass them by readily, if you were not of an inquisitive turn of mind. But those sort of things always seem to catch some boy's eyes, and then investigations follow.   If you dig carefully with a stick, you will soon unearth the burrow, and can generally reach the nest, with its brood of little bunnies. If these are nearly full-fledged, or whatever you call it, they are active little beggars over a short course.

And this is what my two friends had been doing. They had spent the whole afternoon paying domiciliary visits on the rabbits, and exercising their families.   And as they are brimming over with love of animals, I don't suppose that any harm was done, beyond a possible mixing of the families.   They were all put to bed again somewhere, and tucked up safely with earth, to guard them from vermin.   And if you ask where the keepers were, and why such things were allowed to be done, I can only tell you that these two have got round every keeper within five miles of Winchester. Even the crustiest and surliest have given way to their blandishments, and are as children in their hands. In fact, these two of themselves keeper half the preserves of the neighbourhood. They know where all the keeper's traps are, and visit them, in case he should have left an animal forgotten. They pull up all the illegal wires, set in the hedgerows by village poachers, and keep them as trophies. They go round with the keepers to collect the pheasant's eggs, and put them under hens. They are sometimes given his gun, and left for an hour to watch the coops for the wandering sparrow-hawk.

And so their day, except where broken into by the vexatious necessity of being present in the class-room, is one blessed ecstasy of pleasure, and if there is anything that they don't know about the beasts and birds of the woodlands, I cannot think that it is much worth knowing. As for me, I have told you all I know. There is a great deal more besides, for you to learn. I doubt whether there is any limit to the stores of knowledge that nature contains. All that I can hope to claim for myself is to have shown to a few, who did not know the way, the path that leads to the innermost recesses of her heart, which path I have trodden far enough to feel that great heart beating, and far enough to feel sure that, for those who go that way, there is much joy and little pain. Make it your business not to increase this pain more than you can help. I would gladly say never increase it at all, did I not believe that this were well-nigh impossible. But increase it as little as you may. Learn to love and watch. Drink deep of Nature's well, and strive to attune your spirit to hers, so that when the great winds blow, you shall long to shout in one mighty unison with their voices; when the sea smiles, you shall laugh aloud for glee;

and when the aspen leaves whisper in your ear, you shall
listen and understand.   The world is full of fairies still:
they are not dead, but only hidden from many eyes that
have waxed gross.

And so farewell, days of my youth, farewell.
  For all I've said and done that was amiss,
For all I've hurt, for all I've used not well,
  I pray Thee, Lord, to pardon me for this.

And for my youth, for hearing, health, and sight,
  For nights of wonderment and joyous days,
For sea and streams, for down's and wood's delight,
  I give to Thee, Lord of all these, the praise.

And if to any words of mine 'tis given
  To lead young spirits where 'tis safe to tread,
That they may strive to love where I have striven,
  Lay Thou Thy hands in blessing on their head.

Born in a mist of gold, a mist of grey
  Enfolds our footsteps, as we creep to rest:
And well for all, who at the close of day
  Can wonder whether gold or grey were best.

INDEX